The Public Sector Pay System in Israel

OECD

This work is published under the responsibility of the Secretary-General of the OECD. The opinions expressed and arguments employed herein do not necessarily reflect the official views of OECD member countries.

This document, as well as any data and map included herein, are without prejudice to the status of or sovereignty over any territory, to the delimitation of international frontiers and boundaries and to the name of any territory, city or area.

The statistical data for Israel are supplied by and under the responsibility of the relevant Israeli authorities. The use of such data by the OECD is without prejudice to the status of the Golan Heights, East Jerusalem and Israeli settlements in the West Bank under the terms of international law.

Please cite this publication as:
OECD (2021), *The Public Sector Pay System in Israel*, OECD Publishing, Paris, *https://doi.org/10.1787/3b6ad37f-en*.

ISBN 978-92-64-78859-6 (print)
ISBN 978-92-64-80629-0 (pdf)

Foreword

A fit-for-purpose public sector workforce is a fundamental driver of effective governance, and pay policies determine, in part, the ability of governments to attract and retain the workers they need. As such, pay policies are a fundamental part of future-oriented public service strategies, which aim to develop skilled and trusted workforces that can make best use of emerging technologies to address complex policy problems. While pay is not the only reason that people apply for or leave jobs, it is an important factor. Public sector employment and remuneration policies and tools need to keep pace with the rest of the economy.

This report analyses the pay system in Israel's public sector, and provides recommendations to align it with the strategic priorities of the government. It recommends ways to simplify job classification and better match pay to market rates, particularly in areas where the public sector has trouble competing for talent. It also identifies opportunities to better reward performance, productivity and job responsibilities. In Israel, no pay reform is possible without the agreement and active collaboration of public sector unions, and so the second part of this report focuses on public sector labour relations and makes recommendations to improve the functioning of the collective bargaining process in Israel's public sector. This report contributes to the ongoing work of the OECD's Public Employment and Management working party, to support the implementation of the Recommendation of Council on Public Service Leadership and Capability.

The report was drafted by Maya Bacache (consultant), under the guidance of Daniel Gerson, senior project manager in charge of public employment and management in the OECD's Public Governance Directorate (GOV). Donal Mulligan of the OECD Secretariat provided drafting and editorial support, and helped co-ordinate the project. The report benefitted from review by Jon Blondal, Head of the Public Management and Budgeting division (GOV), and from Sandrine Cazes and Chloe Touzet in the Directorate for Employment, Labour and Social Affairs. The OECD would also like to thank Jamie Knights, who participated in the fact-finding mission and provided essential input as a peer reviewer from the UK's Revenue and Customs Agency.

The OECD would like to thank the Government of Israel and the Israeli Delegation to the OECD for their ongoing support and collaboration.

Table of contents

FIGURES

Follow OECD Publications on:

http://twitter.com/OECD_Pubs

http://www.facebook.com/OECDPublications

http://www.linkedin.com/groups/OECD-Publications-4645871

http://www.youtube.com/oecdilibrary

http://www.oecd.org/oecddirect/

Executive summary

Across the OECD, governments spend approximately 9.5% of GDP and 20% of public expenditure in public sector workforce compensation. Events such as the COVID-19 pandemic underline the value governments get for this money: public servants have a critical role in keeping citizens safe and economies functioning. To do this, public sector workforces must be skilled, engaged, and able to plan for and adapt to change. A modern and fit-for-purpose pay system – underpinned by constructive labour relations – enables governments to attract, retain and reward high-value skill sets and talent. This, in turn, contributes to productive and sound public governance.

In Israel, the overall framework for public sector pay has remained substantially unchanged since the 1950s. Since then, globalisation, digitalisation, and socio-economic and demographic change in particular have given rise to new skills needs and work practices, underpinned by new technology. The future of work in the public sector will require the public service to be more forward-looking, flexible and fulfilling to an increasingly diverse range of public servants. This will require a commensurate modernisation of the pay system to attract and retain the talent needed in Israel's public sector and to increase the efficiency of public service delivery. To achieve this, Israel faces a double challenge. The first challenge is to update the pay system while maintaining trust and professionalism in the public sector. The second challenge is to improve bargaining with public sector unions, which exert considerable influence on public sector reform.

In this context, this report examines how Israel's Ministry of Finance can use the public sector wage bill more strategically. The goal is to develop a more flexible, high-performing and outcome-oriented public sector workforce. The report finds scope for (i) reviewing the principles underpinning public sector pay, job classifications and allowances, and (ii) developing a more proactive and constructive approach to collective bargaining to facilitate this. More specifically, the report provides the following key recommendations to the government of Israel:

Rationalise the system of allowances

Allowances are an important component of public sector pay in Israel. Examples include special pay for training, or for car ownership. Many of these allowances are, however, outdated, and no longer correspond to the reason they were introduced in the first place. Now, they are simply perceived as entitlements. Incorporating these allowances into the regular salary structure will make pay more transparent and predictable for both employees and management. It can also help attract external candidates and boost civil service mobility. This rationalisation of the salary structure does not have to affect the overall wage bill.

Identify key competences to align pay with market levels for certain profiles

The public sector needs to be an attractive employer for high-value and future-oriented skill sets that are increasingly in demand in the private sector. In Israel, pay in the public sector is still determined largely by seniority and rigid, outdated pay tables, which makes it difficult to target pay adjustments to attract and retain high-value skills. Linking pay more closely with competences and performance rather than with static factors such as education or seniority would enable targeted pay increases for certain profiles and boost attractiveness and retention.

Simplify the job classification system

A more flexible job classification system in the Israeli public sector would enable greater responsiveness to changes in technology, new ways of working, and unforeseen shifts in operating conditions. Reducing the number of distinct job categories would give greater flexibility to employers to make targeted changes. Revised job profiles that focus on competences is key to embedding greater flexibility, i.e. the understanding that all jobs will and must change their scope. Revising the job classification also presents opportunities to better match pay with market wages for skill sets that are hard to recruit.

Empower line managers to engage in collective bargaining

Collective bargaining does not only focus on wages. It can be a strategic tool for improving working conditions in exchange for management reforms that improve aspects such as flexibility and technological modernisation. This requires increased involvement of line managers and ministries as key partners in the collective bargaining process. They need to be empowered to negotiate with their unions within a well-defined legal and budgetary framework.

Create institutions for alternative dispute resolution

The quality of labour relations is one of the key parameters of a well-functioning collective bargaining system. The frequent recourse to strike action -- and high number of working days lost in Israel's public service as a result -- demonstrates scope to improve social dialogue. Developing viable alternatives to strike action could help resolve conflicts, find agreements within the framework of collective bargaining and thereby strengthen the overall system. Options for mitigating the recourse to strike action could include dispute resolution commissions or independent arbitration and mediation committees. Broadening the range of tools available to social partners to achieve their aims can thus help reduce economic and social disruption.

Limit the scope and timing of strike action to encourage more effective negotiation

Strike action by unions should be seen as a last resort in negotiations with employers. In the Israeli public sector, however, unions have the ability to call a strike with relatively few constraints in terms of motive and timing, whether an existing collective agreement is in place or not. Unlike most OECD countries, Israel does not protect essential services from strike action. Revising the laws and guidelines that structure labour negotiations and strike actions could result in more productive outcomes for government, public employees and the citizens who use public services.

1 Background and Context of Public Sector Pay in Israel

This chapter highlights the characteristics of the public sector in Israel. It discusses the role of the unions in Israel and presents the institutional actors for pay setting and wage negotiations. It also discusses the dual contractual modality across much of the public sector (career-based vs. position-based employment) and the implications this has for delivering on the public service mandate. It concludes with a reflection on the lessons from the initial response to the COVID crisis.

Introduction

OECD countries are facing increasingly complex governance challenges in increasingly uncertain and fast-changing environments. This requires a workforce with the right skills and leadership to find innovative solutions to emerging and persistent policy problems. The future of work in the public sector will require a more agile public sector workforce with new digital capabilities and management systems that adapt to fast-changing circumstances. This requires fit-for-purpose public employment policies, including pay systems, to ensure the public sector is able to attract and retain the right skillsets, and motivate and reward performance.

The Coronavirus (Covid-19) pandemic has underscored the urgent need for flexible and skilled public sector workforces. Across the OECD, the designation of 'essential workers' and large-scale adoption of remote working to mitigate the spread of the pandemic has transformed workplaces and work methods. Public sector workforces are working in new ways, and many changes that were expected to take years occurred almost overnight: for example, dispersed teams, digitalisation of workplaces, and the reconfiguration of management practices. Public sector agencies are learning how to use new technology and tools 'on-the-go', often alongside old procedures and processes. And individual public servants are adapting work and personal time to meet family and caring commitments.

There are three important components to an efficient and effective public service that is able to manage challenges such as the COVID-19 crisis effectively. First, the workforce composition, including skills, competences, values, and motivations, provide the foundation. Second, Human Resource Management (HRM) systems plays a central role in determining the way the workforce is selected and managed, paid, incentivised, trained and promoted. Third, social dialogue and the quality of labour relations help shape an efficient and inclusive public sector.

In 2019 the OECD Council adopted the Recommendation on Public Service Leadership and Capability (OECD, 2019[1]) which codifies these areas across 14 principles for a fit-for-purpose public service. This Recommendation, agreed to by all OECD member countries, presents a normative framework to structure and guide civil service reforms. Pay and effective labour relations are fundamental to many of these principles, in particular the need to attract and retain skilled employees, develop performance-oriented cultures, ensure employee voice, and offer an effective range of terms and conditions of employment.

Box 1.1. The OECD Recommendation of the Council on Public Service Leadership and Capability

Recommendations of the OECD Council make clear statements about the importance of a particular governance function and its contribution to core public objectives. They are based on agreed-upon principles of good practice and aspirational goals. The OECD's governing body, the Council, has the power to adopt Recommendations that are the result of the substantive work carried out in the OECD's committees. The products of such work include international norms and standards, best practices, and policy guidelines.

OECD Recommendations are not legally binding, but practice accords them great moral force as representing the political will of member countries. There is an expectation that adherants will do their utmost to implement a Recommendation.

Adopted in 2019, the Recommendation of the Council on Public Service Leadership and Capability is based on a set of commonly shared principles developed in close consultation with OECD countries. This included a broad public consultation that generated a high level of input from public servants, citizens and experts from around the world. This Recommendation joins a broad range of governance-related Recommendations on themes such as regulatory policymaking, public sector integrity, budgetary governance, digital government strategies, public procurement, open government and gender equality in public life.

The Recommendation presents 14 principles for a fit-for-purpose the public service under 3 main pillars, as shown below:

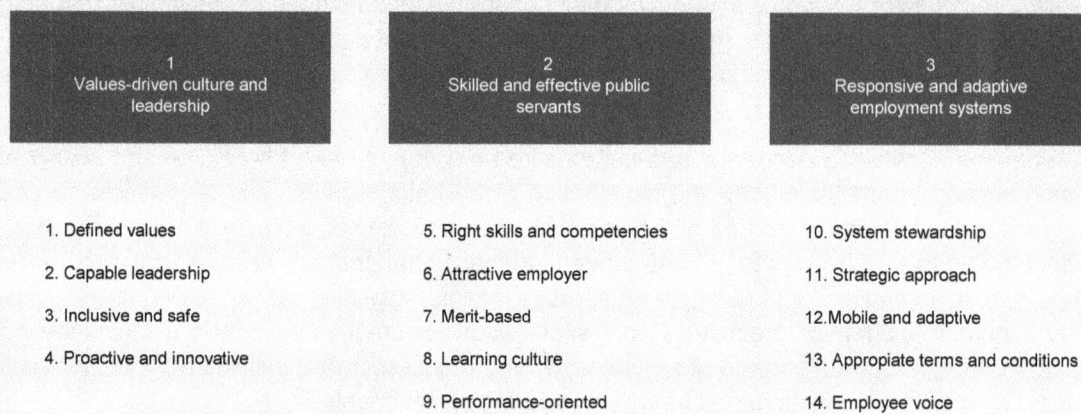

1 Values-driven culture and leadership	2 Skilled and effective public servants	3 Responsive and adaptive employment systems
1. Defined values	5. Right skills and competencies	10. System stewardship
2. Capable leadership	6. Attractive employer	11. Strategic approach
3. Inclusive and safe	7. Merit-based	12. Mobile and adaptive
4. Proactive and innovative	8. Learning culture	13. Appropiate terms and conditions
	9. Performance-oriented	14. Employee voice

Source: OECD (2019), Recommendation of the Council on Public Service Leadership and Capability, https://legalinstruments.oecd.org/en/instruments/OECD-LEGAL-0445

This report looks at how Israel could develop a more strategic approach to pay to attract and retain new emerging skill sets and support a performance culture in the public sector. To achieve these goals, Israel faces two challenges. The first challenge is to update the relatively rigid pay system without jeopardising trust and professionalism in the public sector. The second challenge is to deliver effective public services in cooperation with public sector unions, which exert considerable influence on public sector reform. This report focuses on these two challenges. This first chapter is an introduction that presents the context. The second chapter examines the pay system, its challenges, strengths and recommended reforms. The third chapter addresses the challenges of restoring more systematic social dialogue as a way to reduce labour disputes and increase the efficiency of the public service.

Institutional settings and key actors

The State of Israel, founded in 1948, has no formal written constitution. Instead, a system of basic laws and rights have a constitutional status. The parliament, the Knesset, has passed eleven "Basic Laws".

Executive branch: Ministry of Finance and the Civil Service Commission

In Israel's public sector, pay is determined through collective bargaining. In the public sector, article 29 of the Budget Fundamentals Law gives the Ministry of Finance authority on public expenses, specifically including compensation of public employees. The Minister of Finance has veto power over any agreement relating to wage conditions in a supervised body. Hence, the Ministry of Finance centralises the three functions of budget, pay, and social dialog/collective bargaining. All collective agreements in the public sector are overseen by the Ministry of Finance's Public Sector Wages and Labour Agreements division.

The Civil Service Commission (CSC) is the employer for the central government's ministries and agencies, which makes it the largest employer in Israel. In addition, the CSC is also a regulator of government ministries, determining regulations and procedures related to the recruitment, promotion, evaluation and training of human capital, as well as in the field of organizational structures and standards. The areas of responsibility of the CSC include determining job standards, recruitment practices and the appointment of civil servants, terms of employment, termination of employment and pensions. The CSC is also empowered by law to set ethical and disciplinary standards and procedures, and other rules published in the Civil Service Regulations Code. Through its role, the CSC has developed extensive knowledge and experience, and should therefore be seen as strategic partner in pay reform in the institutions it regulates.

Public sector unions

The right to join a union is established in the Collective Agreements Law of 1957. Union membership is not mandatory, but a representation threshold is reached when a third of employees join a union, in which case even non-members pay the union a service fee and are entitled to all the benefits of a collective agreement. Those mandatory union dues are meant to resolve the 'free rider' problem of employees who get the benefit of the social agreement without contributing to it. However, this method of financing unions is relatively rare. In France, only members of unions pay membership charges. And in the United States, in 2018 the US Supreme Court ruled that unions were no longer allowed to charge non-members.

The General Organisation of Workers in Israel, the Histadrut, dates to the early twentieth century before the founding of the state of Israel and played a major role in the political and economic development of the country. It was part of the labour movement which belonged to the government coalition until 1977. This helps explain the comprehensive system of protective labour legislation and a high rate of union participation. The Collective Agreements Law and the Settlement of Labour Disputes Law in 1957 governs collective agreements. In the 1990s, about 60% of the workforce were members of a union, which contrasts with the decline in union membership in other OECD member countries. In more recent years, the rate of membership in Israel dropped from a peak of about 80% in the 1980s to about 25% in 2012. However, in the business sector, the rate of union membership rose from around 6% in the 1980s to 10% in 2012. In the public sector, most workers (excluding employees under personal contracts and the defence workers) remain unionised.

The Histadrut, renamed "the New Histadrut" remains an important partner in the public sector, coexisting with other social partners such as the Grade School Teachers' Union, the High School Teachers' Union, the Doctors' Union and the Leumit National General Union. In Israel, unions play an important social role and are not only active in labour relations. For instance, the Histadrut used to offer its members social benefits, health services, pension funds, etc. until the 1990s.

Labour courts

The judiciary also plays a key role in this institutional setting. In 1969, the Labour Courts Law created a separate judicial system to solve collective and individual legal labour disputes. The Labour Court System is composed of five Regional Labour Courts and an appeals instance, the National Labour Court. Regional Labour courts have, in equal numbers, members from labour and from management, sitting with professional judges. Labour Courts, since their creation in 1957, are a partner in social dialogue alongside the unions.

Line managers

Another group of important actors in the system are the line managers of ministries and agencies. Although they have little authority to determine pay reforms, they are a central actor in the broader system. There is no successful reform without leadership to effectively manage change. To be implemented and accepted, a reform of the pay system needs political will but also senior and middle managers who support it.

Successful managers require a level of autonomy and authority to make management decisions that impact the operational efficiency and effectiveness of their organisations. When they have the right tools, the skills to use them effectively, and the right enabling environment, managers can negotiate with employees and unions to build buy-in for change and reforms required to develop modern fit-for-purpose organisations.

In Israel, there is an important triangle of power between line management, unions and the Ministry of Finance, and each has a role to play in an effective system to implement successful and accepted reforms. However, the way things are organised today, line managers' roles are rather reduced. This is partly due to a perception that some prefer to act as advocates for their employees vis-a-vis the ministry of finance, rather than as management vis-à-vis the unions. This may in part be due to the fact that some managers are members of the same unions, and covered under the same collective agreements, as their employees, although most higher level manager are employed under personal contracts. In many well-functioning OECD countries, social dialogue depends on a clear distinction between employer (the management) and employee.

Reforms that could help to empower managers could include establishing a common Senior Civil Service for administrative leaders and senior managers, decentralisation of some management authorities, and increased autonomy in allocating the budget. The OECD has developed a Senior Civil Service System model that can be used to guide Israel in this regard. The model highlights two important facets of an effective senior civil service, represented by the two axes of the diagram in Figure 1.1. The first facet is focused on identifying the right kinds of skills needed and appointing people with those skills to the right positions. The second is focused on providing the right management tools, accountabilities and incentives to get the job done. This suggests that it is essential but insufficient to appoint people with the rights skills to leadership positions; they also need a support operating environment. This requires consideration of the incentives and tools available to managers to engage in productive negotiation with employees and their representatives to achieve effective outcomes and reforms.

Figure 1.1. OECD Senior Civil Service System model

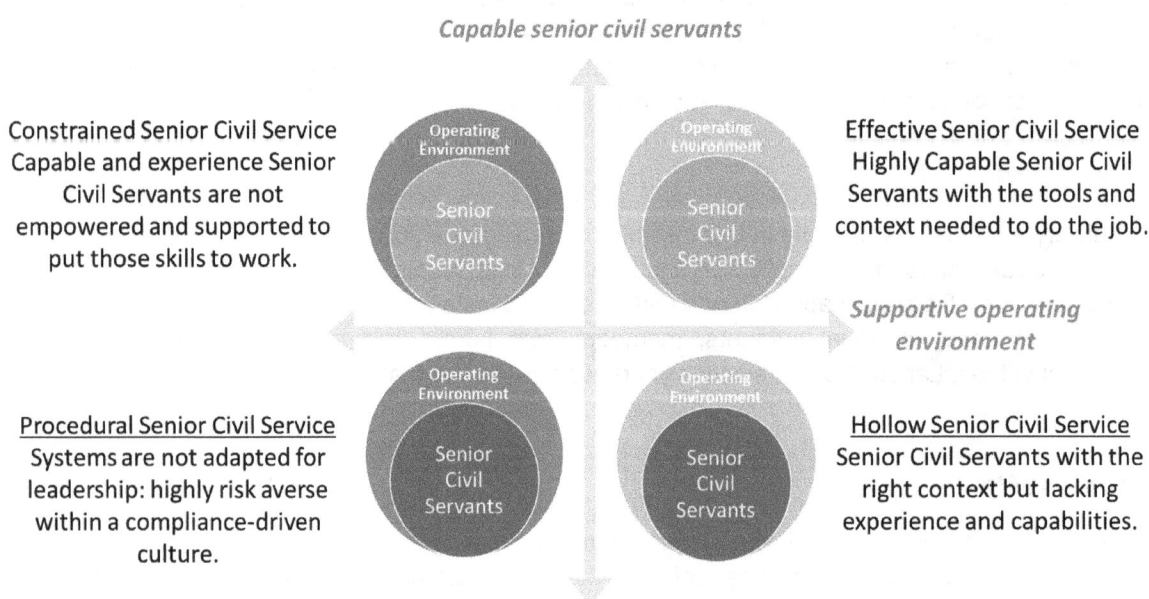

Source: Gerson (2020), Leadership for a high performing civil service: toward a senior civil service system in OECD countries, OECD Working Papers on Public Governance No. 40

Size and cost of public employment in Israel

As shown in Figure 1.2, Israel has a relatively large public sector comprising 19.7% of total employment in 2017; two percentage points above the OECD average (OECD, 2019[2]). The share of public employment has been declining – in 2007 it accounted for 22.6% of total employment, or approximately 700,000 public servants (OECD, 2019[2]).

Figure 1.2. Employment in general government as a percentage of total employment, 2007, 2009 and 2017

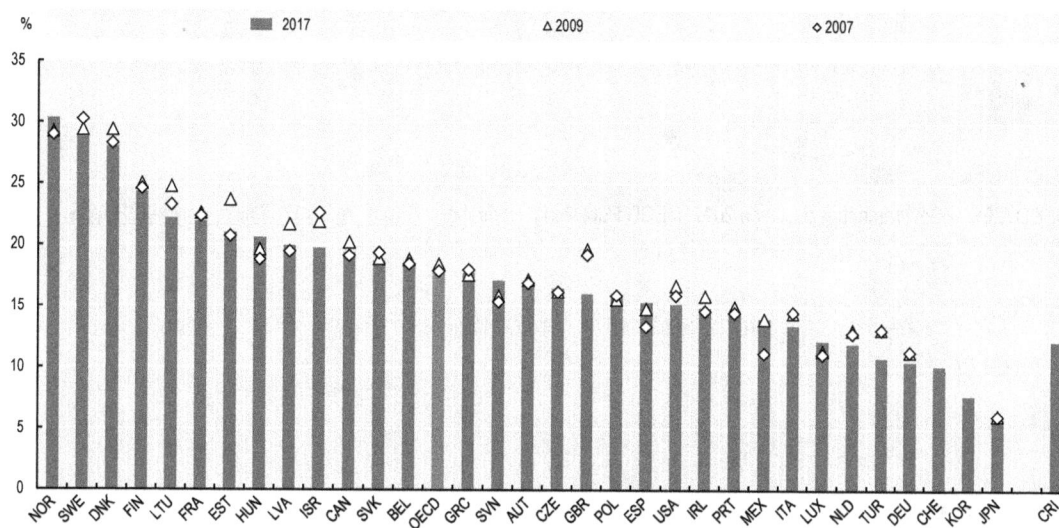

Notes: Data for Japan, Korea, Mexico, Switzerland, Turkey and the United States are from the International Labour Organization (ILO), ILOSTAT (database), Public employment by sectors and sub-sectors of national accounts.
Source: OECD National Accounts Statistics (database).

As shown in Figure 1.3, compensation of government employees in Israel represents 10.4% of GDP and 26.3% of total government expenditure – this is higher than the OECD average of 9.2% and GDP and 22.8% of total expenditure (OECD, 2019[2]). This high share of spending on public employment potentially reduces available funds for other areas, (e.g. public investment, which is below the OECD average) that could contribute to enhancing quality in public service delivery. Compared to 2007, compensation as a percentage of GDP has remained stable, whereas compensation as a percentage of total expenditure has risen slightly, by 1.5% (OECD, 2019[2]). Given this significant investment in public servants' compensation, a central challenge for Israel is enhancing the way this money is spent to ensure it meets strategic goals to attract, reward and retain various skill sets and professional profiles. Public sector compensation can also be a lever for increased organisational effectiveness, e.g. through trading targeted pay increases for the reform of outdated job contracts, or greater flexibility on working hours and location.

Figure 1.3. Compensation of government employees as percentage of GDP (2017)

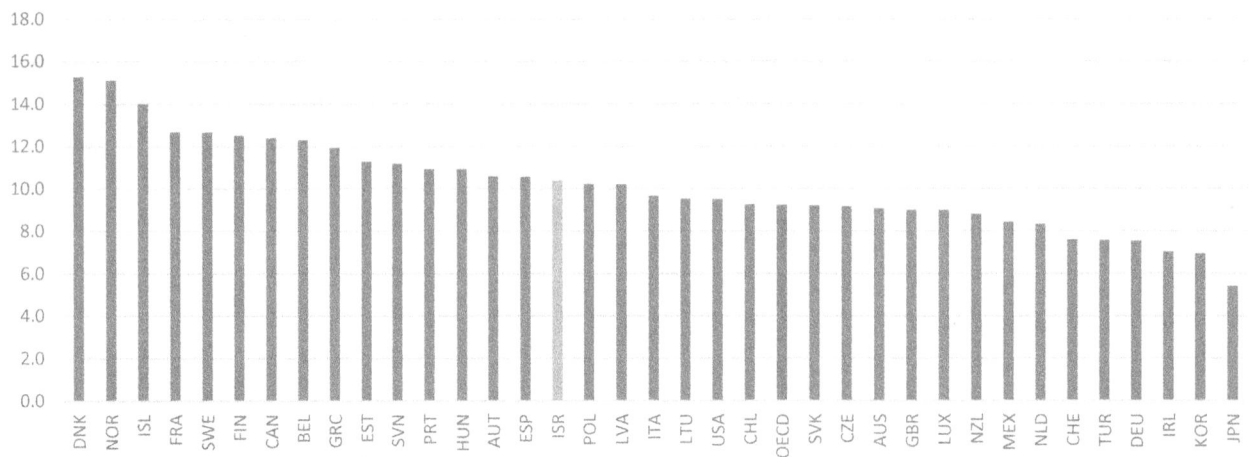

Source: OECD (2017), Government at a Glance 2017, OECD Publishing, Paris, http://dx.doi.org/10.1787/gov_glance-2017-en

Figure 1.4. Compensation of government employees as a percentage of total government expenditures (2017).

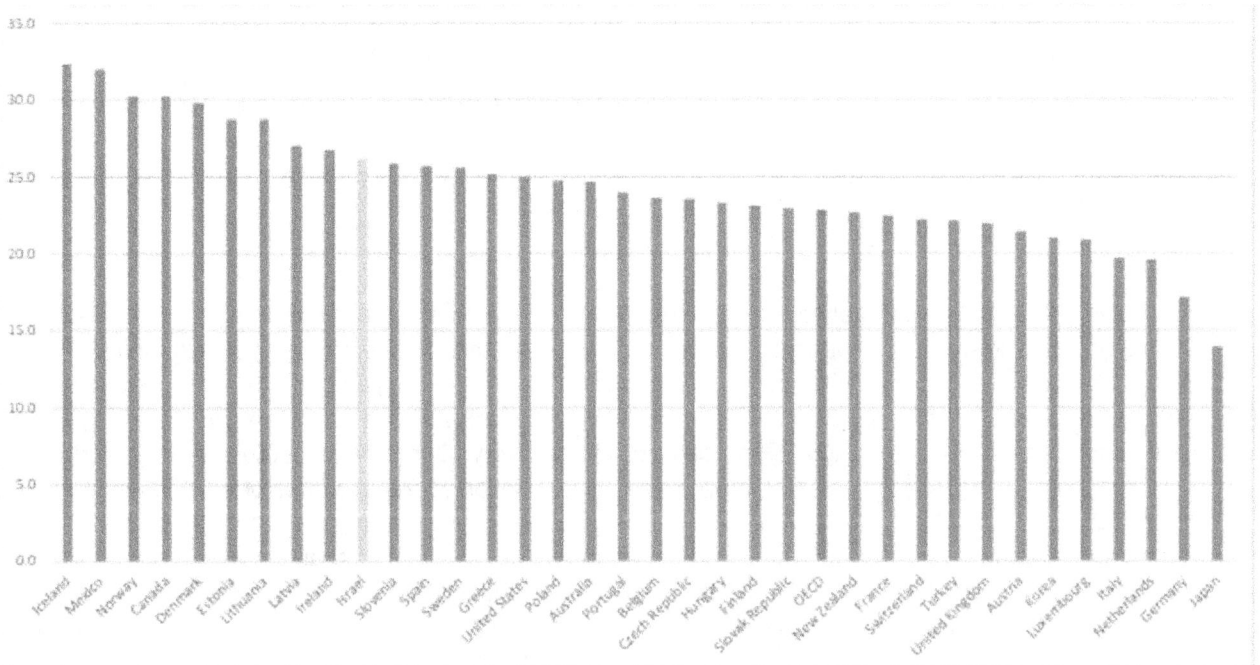

Source: OECD (2017), Government at a Glance 2017, OECD Publishing, Paris, http://dx.doi.org/10.1787/gov_glance-2017-en

Israel's career-based public employment framework

Employment frameworks are the collection of employment policies, terms and conditions that determine how governments recruit and manage their workforce. With many governments experiencing growing pressure to adapt to technological change and compete for desired talent, employment frameworks generally aim to find an effective balance of flexibility to meet changing service needs and security to retain key skill sets.

One way of categorising employment frameworks is to distinguish between career-based and position-based systems (see Figure 1.5). In career-based systems, recruitment is made through competitive selection early in public servants' careers, with higher-level posts open only to public servants. In position-based systems, both internal and external candidates are recruited for a specific post. Israel's system is predominantly career-based.

Both systems have their advantages and disadvantages. Position-based systems can be more flexible and allow the public sector to adjust more quickly when circumstances change. Career-based systems can be better at maintaining cross-government values and a dedicated and independent workforce; however they may be less responsive to timely change and reform. When it comes to pay-setting, career-based systems theoretically emphasise internal pay equity, whereas position-based systems may prove more flexible to match external market wages.

No country has a pure system. Regardless of their initial employment framework, nearly all OECD member countries have implemented recent reforms to balance different needs such as flexibility, openness, transparency and professionalism, common values, and independence. Career-based systems tend to be found in continental Europe, though in France and Germany there is a more recent trend towards position-based reforms. The Netherlands and Sweden are examples of position-based systems.

Figure 1.5. Career and position based employment systems (2016)

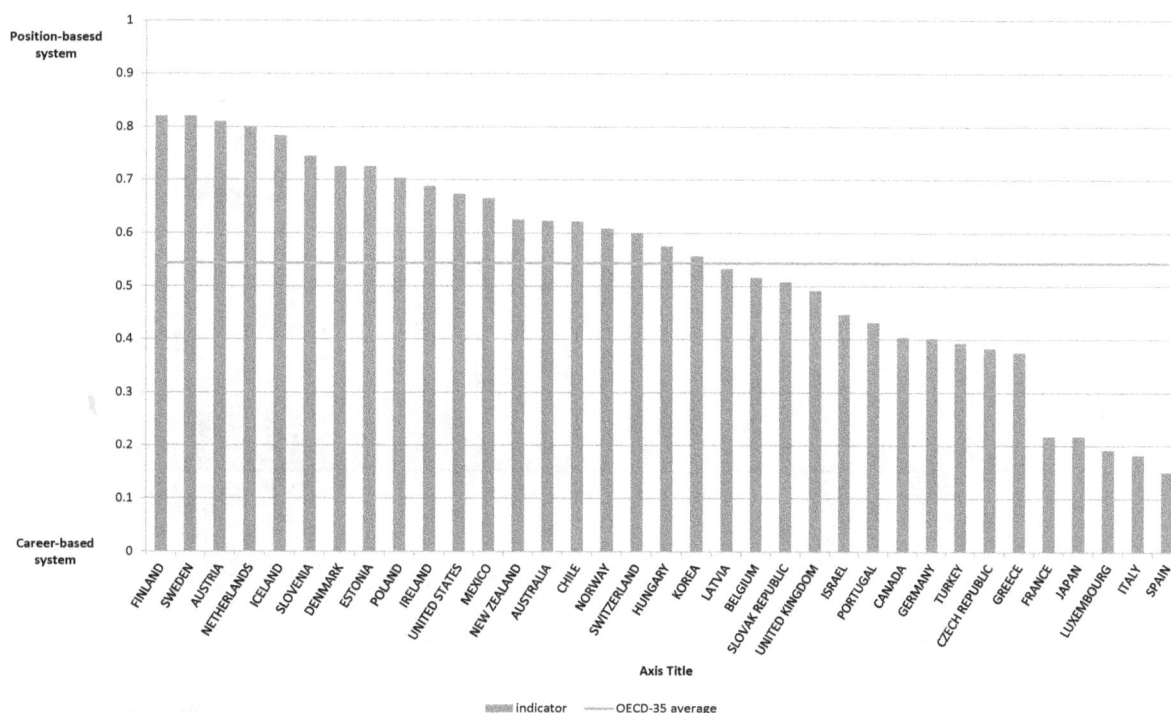

Source: 2016 OECD Survey on HRM in Central/Federal Government, OECD STAN Database.

Another related way of categorising employment frameworks is through the use of civil service status. In continental Europe and South-Eastern Europe, a large share of public employees are employed with a special status under civil service legislation, especially at the central government level – a practice more commonly associated with career-based systems. On the contrary, most North and Eastern European countries use contractual employment under the general labour-law, often based on collective agreements. However, many studies (e.g. (Demmke and Moilanen, 2012[3]) note that, even in traditional career-based systems, the use of labour-law contracts is increasing. Furthermore, there is a tendency, especially in European countries, to apply the status of civil servants only to core areas such as the police and justice.

Most OECD member countries use a mix of these types of contract. Figure 1.6 below shows the distribution of civil servants and other employees across the central public administrations of OECD countries. Civil servants tend to perform different functions (Figure 1.7), have more job security, and different recruitment processes compared to other public employees; however the delineation between these categories varies from country to country. In career-based systems, people working in the category grouped as 'other public employees' may be used for temporary forms of work or for project-based/time-bound work. However, in position-based systems, such as in Nordic countries, other public employees tend to be protected by negotiated agreements that provide them with high levels of job stability and benefits. In France, nearly 25% of public employees do not work under the dominant career-based system, and increasing the number of contractual agents is a reform priority. In Germany, there is a traditional dual system with parallel career-based and position-based systems. Though Belgium has a career-based system, characteristics of the position-based system are found in certain positions, especially for senior management.

Figure 1.6. Civil Servants vs Other Employees in the Central Public Administration (2019)

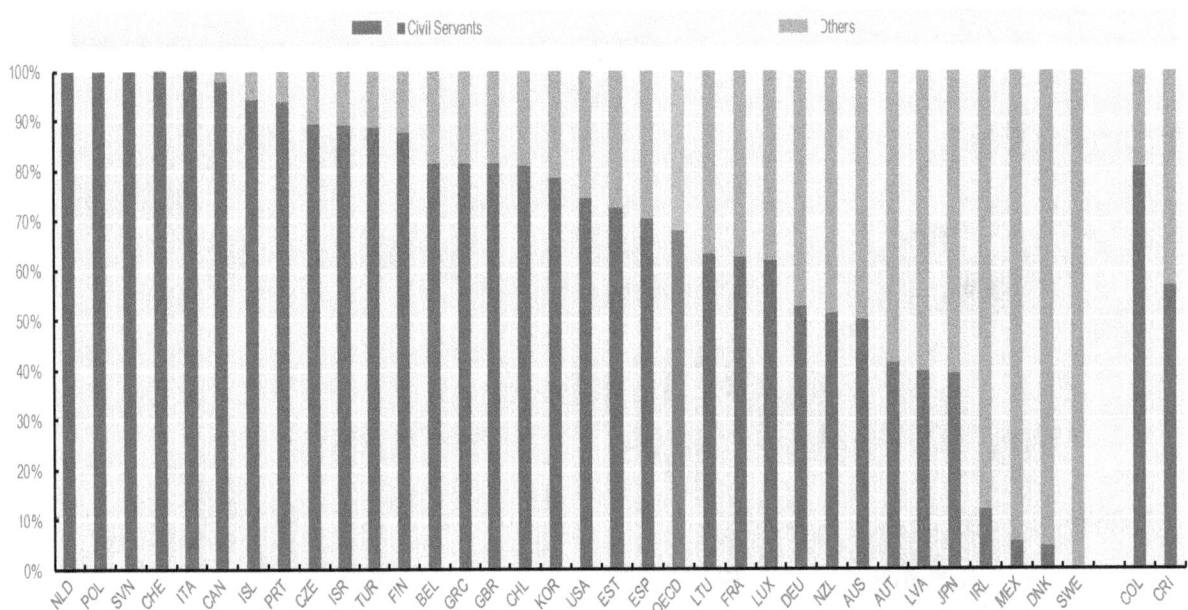

Source: OECD (2019), Government at a Glance 2019, OECD Publishing, Paris, https://doi.org/10.1787/8ccf5c38-en.

A dual system where traditional core functions (such as police and justice) are career-based and services such IT are position-based could be optimal. Positions that require particularly high degrees of independence, and accountability are usually filled by civil servants who have career-based contracts with merit-based recruitment and high job security. Career-based systems are also useful when specific human capital investments are required over the course of a career, such as for teachers.

Conversely, technical jobs, such as an IT programmer required to complete a short-term project, may not need to be employed on a long-term contract if there is no need to invest in her or his skill set the way it would be for a junior civil servant at the outset of their career. When competencies are changing and there is a need for adaptation, position-based contracts can be more flexible and productive.

Figure 1.7. Civil servants and other public employees – common job types (2016)

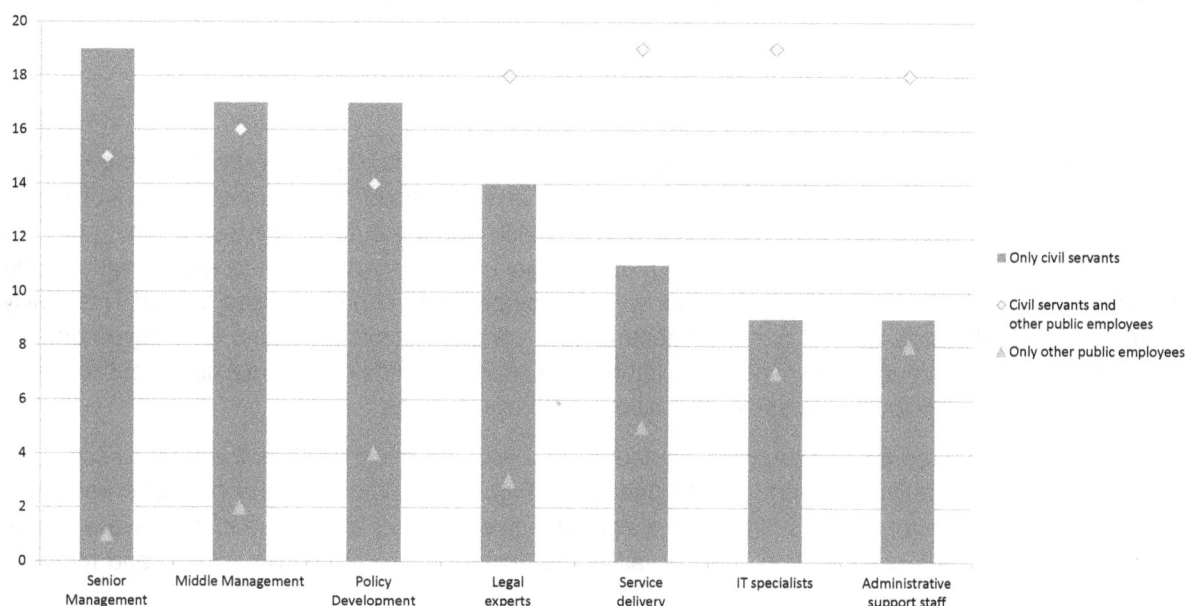

Source: 2016 OECD Survey on Strategic HRM in Central/Federal Government, OECD STAN Database.

'Personal contracts' in the Israeli public sector – an emerging contractual modality

Israel's dominant employment framework resembles a career-based system. Despite certain advantages referred to above, the complexity and scale of career-based systems may act as a barrier to much-needed reforms, such as revising outdated job descriptions or even organisational charts. In Israel, the challenges associated with the broad career-based system led to the creation of a new employment framework called a 'personal contract'. Five percent of public sector employees (around 10% of government ministry employees – see Figure 6) have personal contracts. Employees with personal contracts are mainly professionals such as lawyers, economists or IT specialists.

Personal contracts were meant to give hiring managers the flexibility to recruit staff for specific positions outside the formal scope of collective agreements and to set pay more flexibly. However, following a number of decision by the Labour Courts, after five years, conditions associated with these contracts relating to job security and tenure now converge with those covered by collective agreements, reducing the gains to managers in terms of flexibility. Therefore, personal contracts provide for the same working conditions and constraints as public statutory positions (i.e. career-based).

Moreover, increasing the number of personal contracts over the longer term at the expense of the career-based contracts could also generate a risk of a fragmented internal labour market and inconsistent treatment of public sector staff. For example, workers with different wages may collaborate on similar tasks and share the same working conditions, which may lead to conflict.

The advantages of both systems can be maximised (and downsides minimised) through a clear and transparent set of rules for when and how these contracts are used. The OECD's Recommendation on Public Service Leadership and Capability calls for a transparent set of rules for applying contracts such as personal contracts: the implications for pay, mobility and career are very important in attracting the right talents and need to be known by all applicants. The coexistence of both contract types without clear criteria to apply one over the other may blur the conditions of recruitment and weaken the attractiveness of the public sector and the building of common values among employees, hence reducing trust in the workplace.

Israel could launch a strategic reform to better distinguish the benefits and risks between different contractual types and produce guidelines to ensure consistent application.

Towards an agile public service in Israel: lessons from the COVID response

One common thread linking various public sector reform efforts across OECD countries is the need to embed flexibility and agility in organizational structure and practices while upholding principles of accountability and transparency. The Coronavirus (Covid-19) pandemic has underscored this need for agility and adaptability. New procedures and protocols governing remote working, accelerated hiring processes, and fast-track mobility programmes were developed with unprecedented speed. This agility manifested itself differently across countries depending on specific institutional and legislative contexts and measures taken to counter the pandemic. It therefore provided a stress-test on existing public sector policies and practices, including the salary and labour relations systems.

In Israel, there were three main labour agreements signed with the main union in the Public sector, the "Histadrut", during the first year of the Covid-19 pandemic (Figure 1.8). The main priority of all agreements was to protect public sector workers, and keep them formally employed, as oppose to the private-sector, where at the peak of the crisis in April, nearly half of the workers were temporary laid off and received financial support from social security.

Figure 1.8. Three labour agreements to manage the COVID-19 crisis in Israel

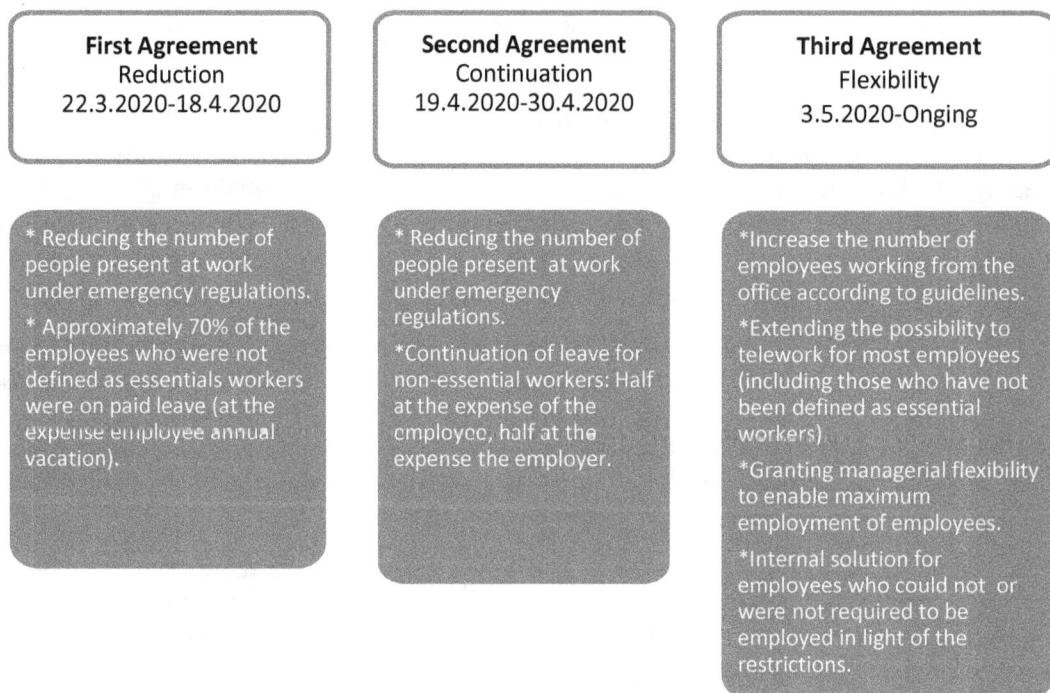

First Agreement Reduction 22.3.2020-18.4.2020	**Second Agreement** Continuation 19.4.2020-30.4.2020	**Third Agreement** Flexibility 3.5.2020-Onging
* Reducing the number of people present at work under emergency regulations. * Approximately 70% of the employees who were not defined as essentials workers were on paid leave (at the expense employee annual vacation).	* Reducing the number of people present at work under emergency regulations. *Continuation of leave for non-essential workers: Half at the expense of the employee, half at the expense the employer.	*Increase the number of employees working from the office according to guidelines. *Extending the possibility to telework for most employees (including those who have not been defined as essential workers). *Granting managerial flexibility to enable maximum employment of employees. *Internal solution for employees who could not or were not required to be employed in light of the restrictions.

Source: Israeli Ministry of Finance

During the first half of 2020 there was a shift in policy: The first two agreements tried to minimize the number of workers in active duty only to those that were essential for keep business continuity. The third agreement, however aimed to bring back all workers and grant employers flexible tools in order to maintain restrictions due to the virus.

The first agreement (22.3-18.4) signed with the Histadrut was intended to ensure minimum business continuity. Therefore, approximately 30%-50% (excluding Health and security sectors) of public workers, those who were defined as Essential Workers, continued to work while the rest were required to use their annual paid leaved. Essential workers were defined as those dealing with the consequences of the spread of the virus or maintaining functional continuity and core services. The Second agreement (19.4.2020-30.4.2020) was a continuation of the first agreement, with vacation days added by the employer.

The Third agreement signed at the beginning of May, enabled the continuation of public service activity in a flexible and efficient manner while addressing the restrictions by the Covid-19 pandemic. According to the agreement, all employees will return to work, except those who cannot be employed in light of the decline in market activity, or in light of legislative restrictions (border workers and so forth). It was decided that employees who could not return to work or whose employment was reduced would be entitled to a special payment. The pay is based on 67.5% of their base salary, to be paid by the employer.

This third agreement required management flexibility to employ as many employees as possible efficiently. In this framework, it was agreed that employers in the public sector will be able to change employee hours of employment (including splitting the work into shifts), adjust the work week, change the definitions and content of jobs, make employees mobile and implement innovative technologies. All this, at the decision of the employer without paying a wage supplement. With the return of many workers that were on vacation from work, teleworking was allowed in order to keep restrictions on the number of people in a room. In most of the public sector, this was not allowed before Covid-19.

Although this agreement is valid for the "corona period", the tools of flexibility provided in it are ground-breaking in the context of Israel's public service management, and will likely enable the public sector to operate efficiently during the crisis, along with providing a flexible response to employees who cannot be employed. This could provide an opportunity for the public sector to expand the management tools in the hands of its managers and continue to operate flexibly even after the period of the Covid-19 crisis. Israel should reflect on the experience of the Covid-19 pandemic crisis to identify new practices that stand to make the public sector more efficient and productive into the future.

References

Demmke, C. and T. Moilanen (2012), *The future of public employment in central public administration*, https://www.oeffentlicherdienst.gv.at/moderner_arbeitgeber/personalentwicklung/international /dokumente/Study_The_future_of_public_employment.pdf. [3]

OECD (2019), *Government at a Glance 2019*, https://doi.org/10.1787/8ccf5c38-en. [2]

OECD (2019), *Recommendation of the Council on Public Service Leadership and Capability*, http://dx.doi.org/OECD/LEGAL/0445. [1]

2 Towards an Effective and Efficient Public Sector Pay System in Israel

This chapter examines the components of an effective public sector pay system and recommends changes to Israel's public sector pay strategy. The chapter begins with an assessment of the relative pay gap between the public and private sector, and follows with an analysis of the job classification system – the foundational architecture of the pay system. The chapter then looks at the specifics of the pay system, how pay is structured and able to attract and retain different skill sets. It considers how Israel's pay system could be better used to motivate and reward performance through performance pay, promotion and mobility.

This chapter addresses the need to design a transparent, effective and efficient pay system in order to equip the Israeli public sector for the future of work. Emerging technologies and changing societies are giving rise to new competences and skill sets to address complex policy problems. Public sector employment and remuneration policies and tools need to keep pace. The OECD has been conducting studies on the future of work in the public service. As a large employer, Governments are adapting their public employment systems to meet challenges of digitalisation, and remain attractive employers for increasingly diverse groups of highly skilled workers. The OECD has summarised these preparations under the following three themes, each with its own implications for pay systems:

- Forward looking: public service employers will need to be better at foreseeing the changes on the horizon and recruiting skills and talent that can adapt. This requires job classification systems that can adequately incorporate emerging skills and attract them with appropriate remuneration packages. It also requires up-skilling and re-skilling to ensure that existing employees are equipped with skills needed to address current and future public sector challenges.

- Flexible: public services will need to be flexible and agile to respond to unforeseen change. This implies the need to redeploy skills to emerging challenges and pull together multi-disciplinary teams across ministries and agencies. Pay systems therefor need to strike a careful balance between specificity for skills and talent, and standardisation across organisations to enable mobility and agility.

- Fulfilling: the diversity of the public service workforce will continue to grow to incorporate more skills and backgrounds. And with diversity of people comes the need for a diversity of employment models and individualisation of people management. This suggests the need to think about pay systems that recognise and reward motivation and achievements, without crowding out intrinsic motivation of public employees.

The government response to the Covid-19 pandemic illustrated the importance of these three factors in addressing modern policy challenges, in particular flexibility. The ability of governments to react to the pandemic largely depended on the degree to which organisational structures and processes were able to adapt to the new and fast-changing conditions. Flexible and fit-for-purpose pay systems are an important component of that change: they enable governments to attract, recruit and reallocate needed skill sets.

Pay systems need to be a fundamental part of a future-oriented public service strategy. The strategy would ideally consider the emerging needs of the public service workforce, and pay would be aligned to support these needs. While pay is not the only reason that people apply for or leave jobs, it is an important factor. However pay in many public service systems is the result of the past, rather than focused on the future. Pay systems were often designed in and for a very different era. Adjustments since then have tended to be at the margins. This is likely due to two main points. First, pay systems need to be stable and predictable, since they form the basis of long careers. This makes large scale change very challenging to do effectively. Secondly, the heavily unionised environments of many public employers requires change to happen through collective bargaining and the many vested interests make it challenging to come to agreements. The last major cross-sectoral pay reform in Israel revised the defined benefits pension plan in 2002. Since then, no other major pay reform has succeeded. Important reforms to the public sector pay system are made difficult by the lack of social and political consensus.

The pay gap between the public and private sectors

Central governments need to engage and retain effective and skilled employees. Pay is a key component of that, particularly in a context where candidates with highly sought-after skills have options outside the public sector to work for the public good. Assuming equal conditions around working hours, location and employment conditions, a difference between the pay in the public sector and the one in the private sector, *i.e.* the pay gap, would be an indicator of the relative attractiveness of sectors.

Since 2008, most OECD member countries faced fiscal pressures that resulted in pay freezes or cuts. In Israel, however, pay negotiations resulted in an increase of pay in the public sector compared to the private: in the last 10 years, pay per employee in the public sector increased by 25% in real terms whereas the increase in the private sector was 11% (Israel Ministry of Finance, 2017). Hence, in recent years the average relative attractiveness of the public sector has increased.

Despite this, the estimates of the pay gap in Israel seem to fit into the global picture of pay gaps in other OECD member countries (see Box 2.1). The average pay in the public sector is higher but this statistical effect usually disappears or even becomes negative when controlled for experience, education or position. The average pay gap is mainly explained by the structural effect; employees are more skilled on average hence higher paid in the public sector.

As such, the primary concern for Israel is not closing the overall 'gap' between the public and private sector: given the relatively small difference in pay, the focus instead should be on targeting pay adjustment for certain professions where there is a marked gap with the relevant market level (e.g. civil engineers), without impacting the overall budget envelope. This is supported by the findings of a recent study conducted by the Bank of Israel which finds that the return on skills is higher in the private sector than in the public sector (Mazar, 2018[1]). This suggests that public sector pay does not compensate workers for their skills in a competitive way compared to the private sector, and a shortage of skilled employees can be expected, everything else being equal.

Pay gaps for specific skills in Israel's public sector

Wages become inconsistent with the competencies one needs to attract if the pay structure does not adapt to social and technological change. In Israel, there seems to be inconsistency for specific job positions. When compared to the private sector, the public sector in Israel pays sometimes more and sometimes less, depending on various factors. Hence, the relative attractiveness of job positions in the public sector varies: for instance, the public sector pays less for new competencies (engineers, digital competencies) and on the contrary, more for lawyers or low skilled administrative workers.

A compressed pay scale (relatively higher pay for low-skill/junior positions, and lower pay for high-skill/senior positions) is common in many public sectors. This impacts the relative attractiveness of the public sector, and lower positions can be very attractive while senior positions much less so. The jobs that are likely to disappear or be transformed in the future are those whose main tasks are simple and routine, where robots and automation can dramatically be efficient substitutes (OECD, 2018[2]). Hence, there is a need to remain attractive for jobs where there are more non-routine tasks and/or which require understanding human actions and reactions in social contexts. These higher-value skill sets are also increasingly in demand in the private sector, which makes it necessary to adapt pay and differentiate it effectively. This is the core challenge of a strategic reform to pay for the future of work.

Moreover, differences can arise between specific employees and at a specific age or specific positions. For instance, compared to the private sector, the public sector pays more for administrative employees but less for public engineers (Israel Ministry of Finance, 2018) resulting in attractiveness issues for engineers in the public sector. It is important to stress that this comparison between averages can cover structural differences in gender, locations or working conditions but is a hint to a need to adapt the pay grid to detailed competencies.

Pay is not the only factor that contributes to attractiveness. Other variables also influence employees' choice of employer, among which are the desire for job security (which may become even more important during economic downturns such as those resulting from the Covid-19 crisis), autonomy at work, sharing common values, serving the public interest, the balance between work and private life, and working conditions. Research from Gallup has pointed to desire for growth and development as a distinct preference for younger candidates (Gallup, 2016[3])). The number of days of work, vacation days and the total number of hours worked also directly impact the hourly wage. By improving talent identification and conditions of work, the government could improve attractiveness. One should recall that the pay gap is only one aspect of the advantages and constraints of a job and that working conditions and institutional rules are to be taken into account to assess the full premium or penalty.

Box 2.1. The Pay Gap in OECD member countries - The economic literature

There are three main challenges to quantifying the pay gap in the public sector. First, it can prove difficult to compare occupations, such as how judges are paid relative to police officers. Second, the definition of pay itself can be problematic, as social security and pensions may differ radically in the public and private sectors. For example, in Israel older public sector employees receive a defined benefits pension plan, which is more favourable than pensions in the private sector

Besides methodological issues, one should be cautious when interpreting the pay gap. One could deduce from a pay gap that there is room for pay freeze or cuts. However, institutional settings affect the spread of wages. For instance, a minimum wage compresses wages at the bottom of the distribution in the private sector. This affects the average gap between the public and the private sector. Moreover, the public employer is expected to behave according to the values of fairness and non-discriminatory practices. For instance, if the average wage is higher in the public sector this could be mostly driven by less discriminatory pay practice whereby there are opportunities for women to earn a similar return for their investment in education and experience as men.

Despite the challenges listed above, the economic literature estimating this pay gap is abundant. Most studies point to a more compressed structure of pay in the public sector than in the private sector, (e.g Grimshaw et al. (2012) on five countries studied: France, Germany, the United Kingdom, Hungary, and Sweden). Pay premium (higher pay in the public sector) substantially reduces and becomes insignificant when composition differences between both sectors' workforce are controlled for. In France, the estimate of the premium, when controlled for various variables, is around between 7% and 15% for women but is insignificant for men. In Germany, there is a premium for female public sector employees between 8% and 19% but no premium for men. In Sweden, there seems to be no significant pay gap. In the United Kingdom, the premium is between 9% and 18% for female workers but not significant for men. When controlled for skill, the pay gap results in a pay penalty for high skilled workers in those countries, and in a premium for low skilled workers. In Greece, Ireland, Italy, Portugal, and Spain pay premium seems to be higher than in other European countries

Some studies even point to the fact that the analysis of the pay gap should take into account the risk of unemployment and the evolution of pay along with the whole career. (Postel-Vinay and Turon, 2007[4])estimate that the wage gap in the United Kingdom is reduced to 0% for individuals with a low risk of unemployment when the whole career is taken into account (including pensions), because of the different wage profiles and different rates of unemployment between the two sectors. Dickons et al. (2012) extend the study on the United Kingdom and analyze earnings profiles along the career in 5 European countries – Germany, The Netherlands, France, Italy and Spain. They insist on the fact that public-private differences in pay are due to the selection of heterogeneous employees into public and private sectors. The pay gap would result of the fact that the public sector selects heterogeneous individuals: according to these studies, the public sector doesn't pay differently similar employees but hires different employees and hence pays them differently.

In conclusion, some specific positions appear to be relatively overpaid and others underpaid compared to the private sector. Hence, a general wage increase or decrease would be ineffective from a strategic perspective. A selective increase in pay would help attract and retain desired profession. Moreover, an update of the job classification, which underpins the pay system, may be needed to better target pay adjustments to specific job positions and competencies.

Job classification: the foundational architecture of pay systems

Revising job classifications is an important step in designing any new pay system. Job classifications distinguish and group jobs, positions, grades and eventually pay ranges. During the hiring process, job descriptions are published to target the specific labour needed. They are also used in promotions, careers, and performance evaluation process. They can be very useful in strategic workforce planning and in identifying training needs.

The design of job classification systems is complex because they must combine flexibility and coherence. A job classification needs to be flexible to fit to the evolving needs of the organisation and the competences available on the job market. However, the classification also needs to be coherent and stable over time. This is because it is a tool for the government to manage promotions, training needs, and implement strategic planning. Moreover, it provides employees with transparency and predictability regarding their pay and career, hence is an important component of attractiveness.

An effective job classification system must find the right level of precision and specification in positions and grades. When too precise, it makes it difficult for managers to adapt a job to changing circumstances, such as the introduction of new tasks, technology or working methods. On the other hand, if too broad, it may not give enough room to differentiate pay according to job characteristics, which may affect employer attractiveness. It may also make it harder to manage career paths. An effective job classification is related to the purpose of use. Hence, the needs of recruiters need to match the job classification system. A one-to-one correspondence between demand and classification has the advantage of precision, transparency, and efficiency in the matching process. However, if the job classification is too narrow, frequent revisions will be needed.

In an economic context where emerging technologies make it necessary to adapt, to learn, to acquire new competencies, end tasks and take in charge new ones, the job classification needs to be rather flexible without threatening employee's security or working conditions. In most OECD member countries (see Box 2.2 for UK and French example), a civil servant is hired under a particular job classification but expects that the role or the working conditions will evolve. Labour law and general agreements specify the constraints that the employee must comply with, but changes in working conditions or the work environment within those boundaries are possible.

Box 2.2. Changing work conditions

In many OECD member countries, various compensation mechanisms allow changing working conditions. For instance in France, public employees who accept a functional or geographical mobility for at least three year are entitled a compensation or bonus. In the same way when the whole unit has to be re-structured or needs to change location, public employees are also entitled a one-time compensation. The amount of this allowance depends on the family situation, the number of years in the position and the distance between the old and the new location. However, some job positions include geographical mobility hence are not open to that sort of compensation. For instance, teachers or judges have a compulsory job and geographical mobility in their career.

Digital technologies drastically affect the tasks that employees achieve and not simply the position. They are expected to alter what employees do but not the objective or the service they provide. Many

---

> OECD member countries have launched this digital revolution in the public sector without necessarily altering the job classification. For instance, the UK launched the Government Technology Innovation Strategy in June 2019 to set out how to use technologies, including AI, in the public sector. It includes a wide program to attract data analysts but also to provide in-house training for public employees. The flexible job classification in the UK allows this functional mobility.

Towards a flexible but consistent job classification system in Israel

The job classification system in Israel is both too specific and too general. Individual job descriptions appear to be extremely detailed leaving no room for modifications that would be considered normal in many countries, such as the rebalancing of work tasks due, for example, to the introduction of new technologies. This requires the public employer to reformulate the job description, which in turn requires negotiation with unions on the terms of the new job description. This gives the union a high level of power to resist managerial improvements and modernisation efforts, which creates unproductive rigidities in the way public employees are managed. Having broader job descriptions that focus on functions and competencies, rather than specific tasks, would enable a more fluid evolution towards modern digital workplaces.

There is an ongoing project at the Civil Service Commission to simplify and reduce the number of jobs in the job classification system in the public sector in order to introduce more flexibility and create margin for manoeuvre.

On the other hand, there is an over-generalisations of job classification for the pay system, which makes it very difficult to effectively target pay to specific job functions and improve competitiveness in the labour market. For example, employees with social science backgrounds are on the same pay scale, but can work in areas as varied as HR, policy development and regulation. In this instance, Israel's public sector pay system does not enable certain functions to be remunerated according to their market value because pay is linked less to job content and complexity than to a checklist of input-oriented criteria such as educational background and years of seniority.

This creates particular challenges given inconsistencies with other job classification systems in the private sector. For instance, in Israel, the private sector distinguishes a civil engineer from an electric engineer and compensates these two occupations differently. Conversely, the public sector does not distinguish between engineering degrees for pay purposes. Therefore, they end up paying relatively more for one type of engineer and less for the other. This means that certain types of engineers, in this case, are less likely to want to work for the public sector.

These examples illustrates a double challenge for Israel's public sector job classification system – highly specific tasks reduce management flexibility, while overly broad pay categories make it difficult to match market value for specific skill sets. Therefore, the goal of any revision to the job classification system should be twofold – to make the specific job descriptions less detailed to enable change and evolution in careers, while, at the same time, making the pay grids more specific to enable different compensation for different occupations, particularly those that are underpaid but in high demand.

Many OECD member countries have experienced these challenges. In the 1990s, many OECD member countries revised their job classification systems (See Boxes 2.3 and 2.4). More specifically, they tried to reduce the number of occupations and to simplify the categorisations in order to gain flexibility. Many also decentralised the classification to specialised public agencies to fit the employer's needs.

The International Standard Classification of Occupations (ISCO) is an international labour classification designed by the International Labour Organisation (ILO) that helps comparison of national job markets. The European Commission has developed a classification of European Skills, Competences, Qualifications and Occupations (ESCO). Only a few OECD member countries follow the International

Standard Classification of Occupations (ISCO-08) to refer to occupations in central government and some have built their own classification closest to their needs. The choice of the appropriate job classification systems depends on the objectives and priorities of the institutions. Since the job classification system implies consideration of the vision for the future, different countries emphasise specific competences or hierarchical structures. Despite differences, these international classification systems can serve as a useful benchmark for Israel.

To conclude, technology evolves, especially in the digital era, and the nature and scope of jobs change over time. Job requirements, contents, and occupations must adapt to this evolving context in order to hire, train, and manage effectively. Drafting flexible job descriptions also implies a profound understanding of what behaviours and competences will be needed in the future. Strategic workforce planning is complementary to a reform of the job classification in order to map existing job classifications and move away from task-based job descriptions toward competency-focused job profiles. Some flexibilities such as technology adaptation are not only related to job classification but also to labour relations which are discussed in greater detail in the next chapter.

Box 2.3. Job weighting to measure and reward job complexity in the United Kingdom National Health Service (NHS)

Job 'weighting' is a component of Job Evaluation (JE) used to assign a numerical value to elements of a job (referred to as 'factors') in order to determine remuneration. Some form of weighting – the size of the contribution each factor makes to the maximum overall job evaluation score – is implicit in the design of all job evaluation schemes. Most schemes also have additional explicit weighting. The rationale for this is generally two-fold. It is unusual for all factors to have the same number of levels because some factors are capable of greater differentiation than others. This gives rise to weighting in favour of those factors with more levels, which may need to be adjusted. It is also the case that organisations place different values on different factors, depending upon the nature of the organisation.

The model used in the NHS has a maximum of 1,000 points available. The number of points available for each factor is distributed between the levels on an increasing whole number basis. Within the available maximum number of points for the scheme, the maximum score for each factor has a percentage value, the values being the same for similar factors. The allocation of total points to factors is set out below.

- Responsibility: 6 factors: – maximum score 60: – 6 x 60 = 360 – 36% of all available points in the scheme.
- Freedom to act: 1 factor: – maximum score 60: – 1 x 60 = 60 – 6% of all available points.
- Knowledge: 1 factor:– maximum score 240: – 1 x 240 = 240 –24% of all available points.
- Skills: 4 factors:– maximum score for each 60: – 4 x 60 = 240 –24% of all available points.
- Effort and environmental: 4 factors: – maximum score for each 25: – 4 x 25 = 100: – 10% of all available points.

Source: NHS

> **Box 2.4. Job classification in France**
>
> France modified its job classification in recent years to adapt its workforce to the strategic vision and needs of the public sector. In 1988, France adopted statutory measures to improve the status of teachers and nurses, which raised their basic wage without leading to a general increase in public wages. In 1990, France renewed the whole job classification system and pay grid to improve career and pay for the least paid workers, and to take into consideration new skills and responsibilities at the other end of the pay range. It was possible to link pay to a specific job position and not only to pay grid thanks to an additional pay attached to positions and called "bonification indiciaire".
>
> The new job classification system that has been implemented in 2006 in France is called "le repertoire interministériel des métiers de l'Etat". It identifies and describes each position or métier. It names and quantifies the necessary jobs within a service; controls for the match between the classification and post; supplies with a reference table of skill to accompany recruitment, mobility, and training; guide and organize the competition for a job position both in external and internal recruitment. In order to increase the efficiency of this job classification, tools were developed: a dictionary of competencies that include formal diploma, knowledge but also social skills and know-how skills; an inter-ministerial job exchange platform; and a mobility kit to help both recruiters and employees to increase mobility.

Transparent and simple pay setting

Designing pay systems around an appropriate job classification system requires a careful assignment of the factors that are used to determine pay. The factors that are used to determine pay refer to aspects that can be based on

- inputs, such as level of education, skills and competencies, previous experience;
- job characteristics, such as skills requirements, level of responsibility, specific job demands (e.g. physical danger, working time, etc);
- outputs such as performance and productivity.

These factors can apply to various structural components of pay, including base wages and any additional payments such as allowances or performance bonuses. This section looks aligning pay more closely to job characteristics and performance, and at rationalising the complex pay structure.

Using job characteristics to set pay levels

A strategic pay system would use pay to attract, develop, retain and motivate the competences the government needs in the future. In Israel, the pay system mainly rewards education and seniority, rather than specific competencies, responsibilities or management skills. Basing pay on broad inputs related to education and seniority limits the link to productivity and effective service delivery. On the other hand, if the job classification is too narrow, pay must be raised at the smallest change in job requirement, which is not only difficult to manage but weakens the ability to adapt to change (see discussion in the previous section).

An additional challenges in Israel is that pay is determined not only by the job classification but also by relative pay in other job classifications. This means that an increase in pay for one specific job position results in disproportionate effects both in the short term (wage) and in long term (pension) through automatic global increases through the whole pay grid. The challenge in Israel is to disaggregate the web of social agreements and the pay grid so that a case-specific intervention on a job position does not result in automatic and global effects.

One option would be to move from pay tables based solely on education and seniority to pay tables based also on specific professions, grades, responsibilities and competences, such as outlined in Box 2.5. A pay system based on job characteristics would also enable employers to adjust compensation for specific groups (if under market value) without impacting the compensation of others (who may already receive above market value).

In the UK civil service, government departments have delegated authority to set pay and terms and conditions of employment for junior grades, subject to compliance with some controls. These controls include the Annual Pay Remit Guidance which sets the parameters for departments making pay awards. This includes the ability to make a business case to make a pay award that is higher than the Pay Remit Guidance allows. A business case can address one of the following criteria: (i) transformational workforce reform; (ii) recruitment and retention issues; and (iii) when transferring funds for bonuses – 'non-consolidated pay' – to the regular pay envelope (Cabinet Office, 2020[5]). This could present an interesting model for Israel to explore. However, this would be a large reform and that would require careful design (and change management) based on discussion with all stakeholders including politicians, leaders, managers, employees and their unions.

Box 2.5. UK Civil service Pay and senior civil service

There is no one unique pay system in the UK. The Cabinet Office has responsibility for the overall management of the Civil Service. It is responsible for publication of the Civil Service Pay Remit guidance (covering the pay of junior Civil Service grades) and ensuring that it is affordable and flexible enough for all relevant departments to apply within their budgets. Pay for senior grades is set centrally through annual Senior Civil Service (SCS) pay guidance based on recommendations from an independent pay review body, the Senior Salaries Review Body. HM Treasury has overall responsibility for the government's public sector pay and pensions policy, and maintaining control over public spending including with regards to departmental spending. Departments have responsibility for implementing Civil Service pay policy for their workforce in a way that is consistent with the Civil Service pay guidance but also reflects the needs of their business and their labour market position. All pay remits must be approved by a Secretary of State or responsible minister, and each department, through its accounting officer, is responsible for the propriety of the pay award to staff.

Each agency or department designs its own pay scale for junior grades in order to match its particular needs. The basic salary is linked to an "individual's value to the organization" measured by job weight/grade. There are usually 7 grades in each department as well as three senior management grades (the pay ranges in the latter are set centrally by the Cabinet Office). Hence it's not automatically given by a pay scale related to education or experience, but depends on various variables that reflect the "size and challenge of the job; professional and leadership competence; an individual's market value".

In 2008 a report to the cabinet Secretary advocated reforms to improve senior civil service. It pushed forward a new reward model that differentiates pay in five items, base pay according to a job classification, pension, an additional pay relative to job weight, content and responsibility, a premium for scare skills and expertise and bonuses to reward performance. The basic wage rewards education and competencies and has 4 to 5 grades to reward experience.

A complementary approach could be to expand the use of shorter-term contracts to specific positions. In 2015, the Israeli government decided to employ most senior levels of the civil service (DGs and some deputies) with time-bound contracts, limiting their duration to no longer than 6 to 8 years. The purpose of this reform was to create a competitive environment for senior employees since these contracts enable higher salaries to be paid for in-demand skills, as well as inducing a higher turnover rate in senior management, thereby creating more dynamic organisations. This is in line with good practice in many OECD countries. The reform included a limited number of positions, which account for less than 1.5% of all positions in the Israeli government. The Israeli government could consider expanding this employment model to some additional high-level management jobs or to specific technological positions, for example.

Simplifying the pay structure, rationalising allowances

Pay structure refers to the balance of the base wage and any additional payments, regularly paid (e.g. allowances for specific aspects of the job) and not regularly paid such as bonuses for performance. While some additional payments will be necessary to compensate for special features of some jobs and enable some level of flexibility in the across the pay grids, it is generally preferable to structure pay so that the base wage is as large a proportion as possible. This helps to ensure that pay is transparent, fair and easy to manage. Nevertheless, additional payments can make up sizeable portions of the public sector wage bill. For example, in the central public administrations of Italy, Spain, and France, additional payments may represent up to 30% of the gross wage, and sometimes 50% especially for senior positions or highly ranked managerial positions.

The share of additional payments in Israel is high. On average basic wage is only around 46% of total compensation for general government civil servants, with a lowest share of 28% in the health system where doctors can have additional pay in the private sector, and a higher share of 80% in the education system.

Simplifying the existing pay structure would be a useful exercise to increase transparency for both employees and employers. On top of the base salary, many additional payments depend on factors such as experience, location, and family situation. These allowances are usually the result of collective bargaining processes, and therefore tend to be incremental changes that may be applied unevenly based on the strength of the union, rather than the result of strategic decisions taken by the government to build an effective public workforce. Over time, these various components are added to, increasing the complexity of pay across different job categories.

This complexity blurs information on pay for a specific job positions, and lack of transparency limits recruitment and mobility. In Israel, it is difficult for recruiters to advertise the specific pay of a job because it is context-specific – it depends on many factors including the particular situation of an applicant. This makes it very difficult to advertise pay information in recruitment campaigns and attract good candidates. This also affects internal mobility, as civil servants may not be able to easily identify potential remuneration for another position in a different Ministry or agency, for example. Removing various allowances from collective agreements could make funds available to raise base salaries in positions which are currently under-paid.

Allowances are an important component of public sector pay in Israel, valued in many cases by employer and staff alike for their link to motivation and engagement. However, many allowances are the result of labour negotiations from a long time ago, and may now be disconnected from the reasons why they were implemented in the first place. For instance, the car allowance would be a potentially useful candidate for rationalisation: initially designed to compensate employees for the cost of using a car and to improve working conditions, it resulted in an incentive to buy and own a car instead of using public transportation. This now contributes to pollution, traffic congestion, and a requirement to provide parking. Other additional payments that could be theoretically efficient have been expanded to more workers than needed, creating a paradox of aggregation. For instance, readiness pay is paid to workers available after working hours and might be less relevant nowadays, except for only specific professions.

Training allowances are another candidate for modernisation. These allowance are attributed to employees for acquiring new skills, however the list of specific courses dates to collective agreements from the 1970s and are outdated, therefore they don't always match with the needs of employers. Though the initial purpose of those training rewards was to increase incentives for employees to invest in their competencies, this situation today results in perverse effects: employees are less willing to accept other learning opportunities that do not open the right for new allowances; components of wages are fixed without the employer's evaluation; and mobility between positions is reduced because pay is not linked to job position. Training in some cases appears to be seen less as an essential component of life-long learning, and more as an inconvenience to be offset with concessions from the part of the employer. Therefore, Israel should carefully review these payments which no longer appear to meet the objectives for which they were designed.

Lifelong learning is essential to evolving in one's career, to adapt to technological changes and to respond to citizens' needs. Well-designed and adapted learning programmes are essential and need to be preserved, evaluated regularly, and upgraded. The issue is to implement the right set of incentives to both employer and employees to reward learning. In theory, there is no need to reward training by an allowance. If training is effective, it increases performance hence it should enhance career development and increase wages. Rarely do OECD countries rely on direct financial payments to motivate staff to undertake training. Rather, to increase individual learning incentives, training is often linked to performance management processes, to ensure that civil servants receive the training they need to perform and progress in their careers, and that training provision is effectively coordinated. Mentoring, peer learning and mobility assignments can also help to promote learning. Hence, Israel would benefit from rethinking its training incentives and reducing the direct link between wage and hours of training.

To summarise, there is significant scope to streamline the structure of the pay systems and significantly reduce the number of allowances. The simplification of the pay structure (base wage, additional payments, working time, benefits) is the first step for transparency, and hence an efficient and inclusive pay system. Additional payments that are historically set do no longer fit their purpose and are not an efficient way to increase pay. The pay system needs to rely not only on education and seniority but also managerial responsibilities, relative pay to the private sector and working conditions. The adaptability of the pay system is a necessary condition to adapt the workforce composition to public service delivery needs. Some OECD countries have established independent pay review bodies to provide recommendations on pay in line with strategic priorities (Box 2.6).

Box 2.6. Independent pay review bodies

Ireland: In 2016, the Irish Government approved the establishment of an independent Public Service Pay Commission (PSPC) to advise Government in relation to public service pay. The Commission comprises a Chairperson and seven members, all of whom were appointed by the Minister for Public Expenditure and Reform. The Commission produces a series of reports providing recommendation to government on various aspects of how pay affects attractiveness, recruitment and retention.

United Kingdom : The Office of Manpower Economics provides an independent secretariat to the following eight Pay Review Bodies which make recommendations impacting 2.5 million workers (around 45% of public sector staff) and a pay bill of £100 billion: Armed Forces' Pay Review Body (AFPRB); Review Body on Doctors' and Dentists' Remuneration (DDRB); NHS Pay Review Body (NHSPRB); Prison Service Pay Review Body (PSPRB); School Teachers' Review Body (STRB); Senior Salaries Review Body (SSRB); Police Remuneration Review Body (PRRB); National Crime Agency Remuneration Review Body (NCARRB).

> **United States:** Under the Federal Employees Pay Comparability Act of 1990 (FEPCA), the Federal Salary Council makes recommendations on Federal pay. In 2019, these recommendations covered estimated locality rates; the establishment or modification of pay localities; the coverage of salary surveys conducted by the Bureau of Labor Statistics (BLS) for use in the locality pay program; the level of comparability payments; and the process of comparing General Schedule (GS) pay to non-Federal pay.

Performance-related pay

Performance-related pay (PRP) systems link pay bonuses and/or increases to defined performance indicators. The effectiveness of PRP systems depend on system design and organizational context. Five key aspects need to be taken into consideration when designing PRP systems:

- Defining performance: clear and measurable targets evaluated through excellent performance appraisal systems

- Time horizon: short-term or long-term incentives, based on periodic performance appraisals

- Size of the incentive: establishing a motivational incentive while preventing unintended consequences

- Probability to receive an incentive: how common should it be to reward high-performing civil servants

- The recipient: individual or group-based reward

Linking pay to performance is intended to motivate employees, and to compensate them for exceptional effort. However, public sector employees are often highly skilled professionals who work in an environment where performance is difficult to measure. Hence, the evaluation procedures need to be consistent with employee's aspirations, intrinsic motivation and willingness to perform. When the wide objectives of the institution match employees' personal objectives and when the quality of management is well perceived, then, PRP is more likely to be effective. In Israel, the current pay system does not appear to enable managers to effectively reward talent and performance.

If nearly all OECD countries have implemented some form of PRP, few have succeeded in designing an effective system of bonuses. Studies have reported weaknesses in PRP in the public sector and little evidence for increased motivation or increased quality of public services. The small share of bonuses in total compensation, the complexity of performance assessment, and the multitasking problem are commonly reported difficulties. Nevertheless, the PRP can be useful in raising and signalling performance norms across public sector organisations.

Overall, in OECD member countries, there is high diversity with no clear best practice PRP. However, a number of principles that make up a good PRP system include:

- Perceived legitimacy – a PRP system only works if employees and employers agree that it rewards the right people for the right things. This suggests the need for simplicity and transparency, for differentiation of rewards.

- Alignment of criteria between individual performance and organisational results – PRP should reward people whose working behaviour is conducive to achieving organisational objectives. However getting this link right is very challenging, especially when organisational objectives rely on collaboration, and when the organisation is working in uncertain environments where simple production of measurable outputs is not necessarily aligned to the achievement of desired outcomes.

- Tools to deal with low performance – discussions of PRP usually focus on the reward for the top group, but equally important is how to deal with those that receive low performance ratings. If managers don't have tools and incentives to manage their low performers, then they will often hesitate to use the performance system at all.

The perception of the PRP system is a key factor in its success. When perceived as controlling, it crowds out intrinsic motivation. However, when perceived as supportive it could complement and reinforce intrinsic motivation. Wenzel et al (2017[6]) show that a "fair, participatory, and transparent design" may both reduce the complexity cost of a PRP system and foster the intrinsic motivation of employees. Fairness is an important factor in the implicit contract behind the PRP system. A PRP system is perceived as fair when performance pay is not based on random performance ratings and there is a direct link between the amount of performance pay and the perceived quality of performance. A pay system may be perceived as unfair if performance pay is based on favouritism, on flawed performance evaluation systems, or on a system that results in low levels of differentiation – i.e. a low level of pay bonus.

PRP systems earned an important place in most public sector reforms since the 80's. Two-thirds of OECD member countries use PRP for government employees (OECD, 2005[7]). In France, Canada, and New Zealand, PRP is primarily used for senior managers, whereas in most other OECD member countries PRP applies to most public employees. Israel has implemented PRP that targets mainly non-managerial employees. As indicated in Figure 2.1, on a composite indicator that measures the extent of the use of PRP in central government, Israel makes more extensive use of PRP than other career-based systems like France or Spain.

Figure 2.1. Extent of the use of performance-related pay in central government (2016)

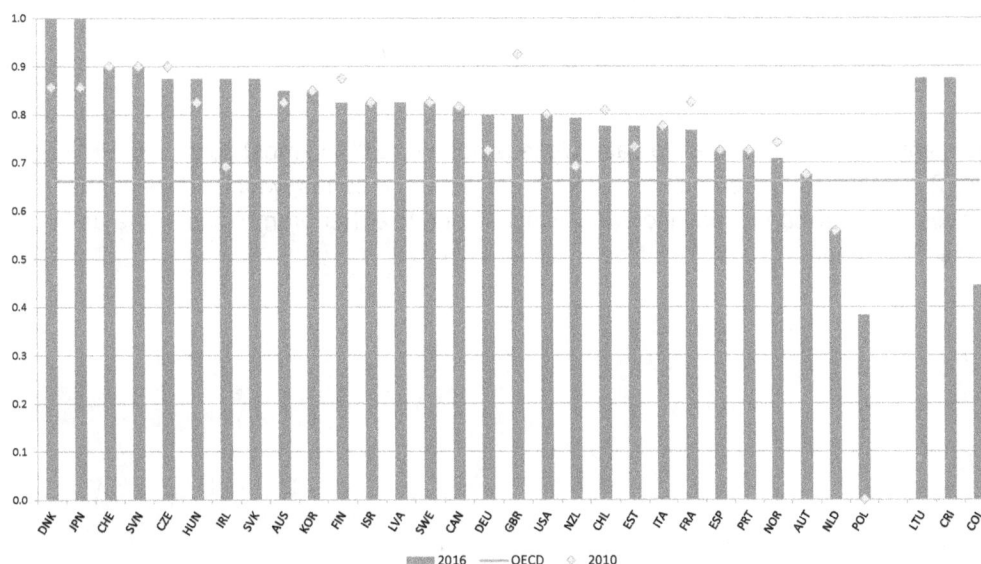

Source: OECD (2017), Government at a Glance 2017, OECD Publishing, Paris http://dx.doi.org/10.1787/gov_glance-2017-en

Performance assessments are used in all OECD member countries, except Iceland and Norway, for nearly all public employees. However, there is an important heterogeneity among OECD member countries in the way performance is measured, assessed and translate into pay. Like in Israel, meetings with superiors or written feedback from superiors are usually held once a year and 360° evaluations are rarely used. The performance criteria used in Israel looks like the criteria used in all OECD member countries (Figure 2.2). However, in other OECD member countries, the choice and use of the criteria are usually decentralized to local institutions and departments. This decentralization allows the criteria to meet the needs and specificity of the sector and organisational environment.

Figure 2.2. Performance criteria used in public organisations (number of OECD countries)

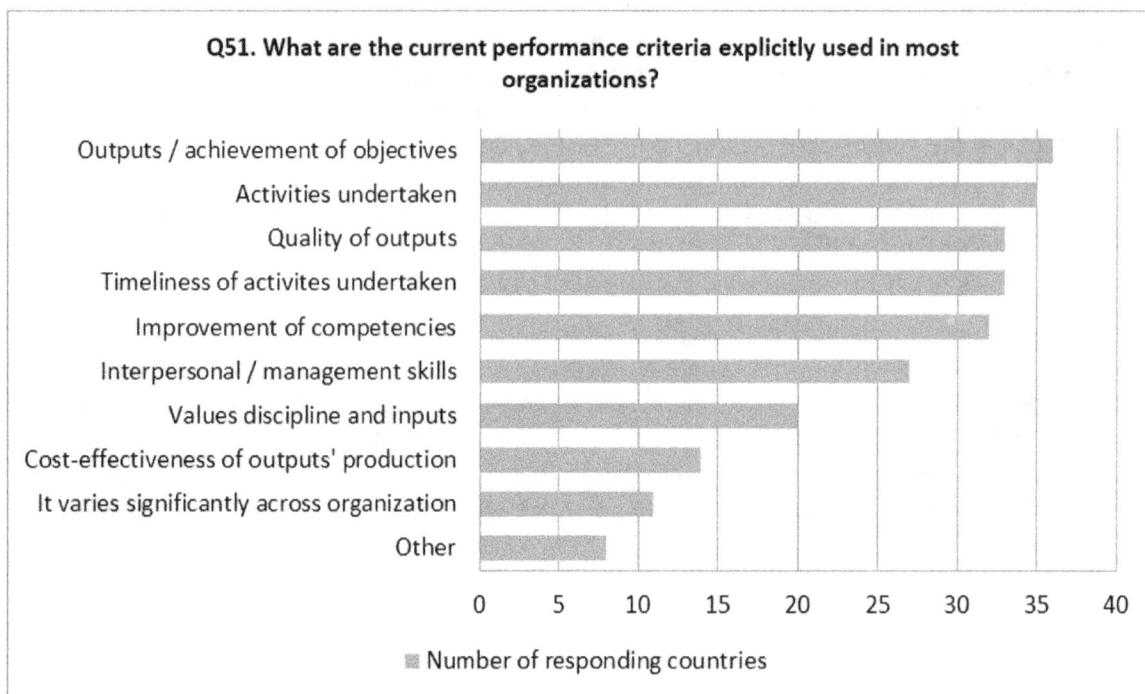

Q51. What are the current performance criteria explicitly used in most organizations?

Source: OECD (2016), Survey on Strategic Human Resource Management

The maximum amount of PRP related to base wage is not over 20% in most countries. PRP takes various forms (Figure 2.3), and most often either a one-off performance bonus, which corresponds to the idea of giving incentives, or a permanent pay increase, which is due to either promotions or the use of PRP as an increase in the base wage.

Figure 2.3. Types of performance pay used in OECD countries (number of OECD countries)

Q116b. Do organizations mostly use:

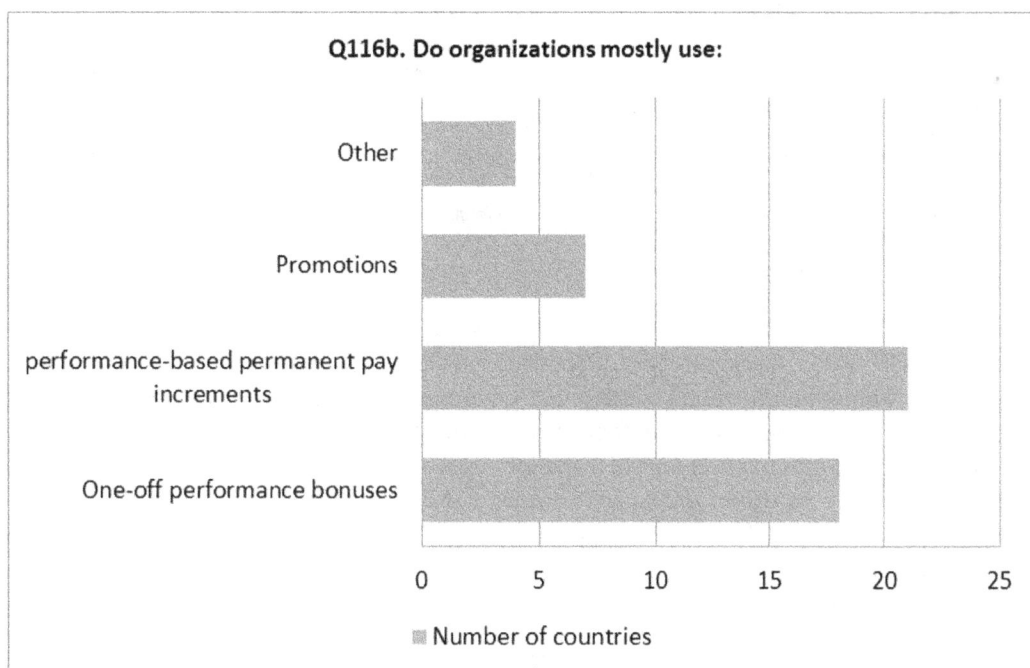

Source: OECD (2016), Survey on Strategic Human Resource Management

In Israel, various forms of pay for performance were introduced after a collective bargaining agreement signed in the late 1960s (the 1969 collective agreement on incentive pay) and includes premium payments, premium in training and premium on leave. In 2017, about half of the 72,000 employees who work in government offices and hospitals were eligible for bonuses linked to performance, and of those, about 95% received 95-11% of the maximum amount of their possible bonus (Israel Ministry of Finance).

Box 2.7. Challenges to implementing performance related pay in the public sector

- **The complexity of the public service 'good'**: Public services generate a multitude of outcomes, some of which are more easily measured than others. In addition, the ultimate outcomes of many public sector activities may only be visible in the long-term, raising questions about the feasibility of accurate and meaningful performance measures within a PRP scheme.

- **Multiple principals**: The public sector involves a wide variety of potential 'owners' and stakeholders (service users, managers, unions, professional bodies, the Government, taxpayers). Any PRP scheme in the public sector must be capable of reconciling the variety of outcomes from these multiple stakeholders and interests.

- **Multi-task problems and collaborative activity**: The delivery of public services tends to be a complex and inherently collaborative activity. Attributing individual responsibility for performance and outcomes may therefore be challenging, and individual incentives could mitigate against team work.

- **Misallocation of effort**: PRP schemes may incentivise outcomes which are more easily and directly measurable (OECD, 2009), encouraging employees to focus on these outcomes at the expense of others, e.g. 'teaching to the test' in education.

- **Gaming:** When performance indicators become 'high stakes' employees may attempt to game the system (Neal, 2011), where workers seek to maximize their gains while minimizing effort or without increasing performance. This can lead to significant problems in the public sector, where outcomes can have a wide social impact.

Source: The Work Foundation (2014), *A review of the evidence on the impact, effectiveness and value for money of performance-related pay in the public sector,*
https://assets.publishing.service.gov.uk/government/uploads/system/uploads/attachment_data/file/381600/PRP_final_report_TWF_Nov_2014.pdf

Israel's original PRP was not intended to reward individual performance. At the beginning, the measurement of performance was made at the group level and the variable pay was addressed to the unit. This kind of collective incentive can be effective when the performance is difficult to measure at the individual level or when collaboration is crucial in the job position. Collective rewards tend to increase group cohesion and cooperation between employees, but do not increase individual performance and do not attract competencies. Indeed, collective PRP can have a negative retention effect on the most productive employees that would seek more productive groups or a negative effect on motivation for those who range above the average performance.

Furthermore, these group incentives require two conditions to work well. First, there must be legitimate ways of measuring performance, and second, the work these groups do must be comparable to others. This means that this tends to work well in stable operational environments - for example, offices that process drivers' licenses or that deliver specific sets of citizen services in similar ways to others.

In Israel, variable pay was first addressed to work teams with measurable productivity. A committee including management and union representation sets the methodology by consensus, and all stakeholders must agree on any change to the calculations. However, over the years, this has been extended to include administrative and headquarters work as a result of labour negotiations. Determining productivity metrics for administrative positions is particularly difficult (see Box 2.7).

Once set, it is procedurally difficult to change the way performance is measured for each of the groups in Israel's system. This is due to the multiple stakeholders (e.g. management, employees and their unions) who need to agree – each has a veto to any changes proposed. This seems to result in out-of-date performance metrics, which no longer make sense in a modern work environment. Over time, this pay becomes seen as entitlements to be spread around evenly rather than to differentiate and reward genuine performance. Once this happens, unions have little incentive to agree to changes that improve the performance metrics used.

This is not a problem unique to Israel. In many other OECD member countries, pay for performance has become an additional payment rarely linked to effective performance indicators. This misuse of variable pay is counterproductive since it fails to reward performance but also creates frustrations and misaligned expectations. This may be due to various factors, including a lack of managerial capability, institutional settings, and the centralised nature of the PRP process.

Recognising these challenges, a different kind of PRP focused on individual incentives has been introduced into headquarters units. Since measuring performance in services is challenging, a "differential system" comparing relative employee performance has been introduced more recently. This second system appears to be easier to implement since managers don't need to assess very precisely the performance indicators but need only to be able to compare individual employees. This individualised approach can be efficient but may be detrimental in collaborative working groups. If there is a given amount available for a particular group, colleagues could hypothetically take a "zero-sum" approach suggesting that more bonus for themselves requires less for the others. Hence, this gives the wrong incentives to work against colleagues' performance, and risks increasing the level of competition and conflicts in the workplace.

The effectiveness of PRP depends on managers with the right skills and tools to properly assess performance and then manage staff with low performance. When managers have little discretion to address low performance, and when managers fear the social impact or peer pressure of not rewarding someone, PRP can be counterproductive and detrimental to the entire performance evaluation system. In the case of the group evaluation method, managers have no discretion as the performance metrics are set in committee with unions and employees. As mentioned above, this may work well in operational setting with clear and comparative performance metrics. However, it is likely not well suited to many of the work settings in which it is currently implemented – in these cases it may be best to transition to an individualised system with effective managerial support.

PRP may also be badly designed because of institutional settings. Since in career-based systems dismissals are difficult, PRP ends in relative pay increase, hence potential social conflicts, or on the contrary smooth increase for all hence no incentive effects. The performance indicators once decided for remain often rigid and don't adapt to a change in objectives or working conditions. Moreover, managers don't always have the discretion to set bonuses that can be decided for at the centralized level or even by the employee's delegates at local pay committees.

Given the variety in PRP, and given the wide set of undesirable effects in using PRP, it is not possible to recommend an optimal method. Each institution, each department would profit from a PRP system designed for local needs that reflect the employees' values and culture. Decentralization and differentiation in measurement methods and translation into pay are likely to make the whole system more legitimate and flexible, assuming effective controls on abuse are in place. Israel may wish to run a review of all the current arrangements in place with a focus on two objectives. The first is to identify teams subject to the group pay for performance processes which should transfer towards an individual system. This would entail groups which to do not do easily measurable and comparable work. The second focus of the review could be to look at those groups for whom collective rewards make sense, but require updates to their reward mechanisms.

Moreover, decentralization of PRP has another advantage of making the wage bill more predictable. When pay increases are decided at the centralized level, PRP may end in general increase, since the Ministry of Finance can be pressured to increase pay for all since it is the last resort decision maker. Alternatively, the ministry of finance could give a small percentage of the overall wage bill to each agency and allow the management to use it for performance pay as they see fit, with appropriate guidelines in place to avoid abuse. These guidelines usually include mechanisms to ensure transparency, oversight by senior leadership, and peer review. For example, a manager who wants to provide a bonus would need to gain approval from the Director General of their Ministry, and justify their rationale to their peers in their management team.

Targeted pay increase and performance rewards are easier to implement at a decentralized level. For instance, in the UK, individual departments have a budget and decide how to spend it and can target pay rewards to specific positions and employees. Decentralized pay leaves individual managers more flexibility to reward good performers and attract needed skill sets while not impacting the overall wage bill.

To conclude, a pay system should recognise and reward excellence and exceptional performance. Nonetheless, it can be complex to reward performance without jeopardizing intrinsic motivation, trust, and public values. PRP naturally appeals to our sense of justice and can be theoretically efficient, but badly designed systems are abundant, and can be detrimental to employee motivation, team cohesion and organisational effectiveness. An effective PRP system must be perceived as fair by all involved stakeholders – in particular the employees and the managers, and therefore relies on employee buy-in and managerial discretion. Employees and/or their representatives should be involved in the design of the system, but managers need discretion and support to make the system work effectively. However, PRP is not the only way to address the challenge of rewarding performance, and a more flexible pay scale or larger mobility opportunities can be more effective when understood and well-perceived by the employees. Career mobility is also a very effective incentive, which is discussed in the next section.

Box 2.8. The Performance pay system for teachers in England and Wales

In 2013, a new system of performance pay for school teachers was introduced in state primary and secondary schools. The former pay system enabled six annual pay increments by performance-based progression, on the 'main scale'. The objectives of the new system were to introduce the performance element in progression between the main and the upper pay scales, and to better take into account the performance element on the three points on the upper pay scale. The objectives are agreed upon at the start of the school year. Then after mid-year feedback, at the end of the school year, a final assessment contrasts the results on the national teacher's standard and the agreed objectives. The school senior management reviews the recommendation on pay given in the final assessment and decides on the merit-based pay. National school inspectors from the Office for Standards in Education, are in charge of checking whether performance awards are efficiently used

Source: Marsden, D. (2015) *Teachers and performance pay in 2014: first results of a survey*, Centre for Economic Performance, CEP Discussion Paper No. 1,332

Career mobility and seniority

When job classification and pay systems lead to identical or comparable pay ranges for comparable positions, they can encourage employees to move between organisations and units, hence increase mobility. Mobility in the public sector can increase motivation, experience and competency development. Career mobility can be an effective way to reward talent and performance. In Israel, given the small share and use of individual performance related pay (PRP), promotions are an important way to incentivize effort. When promotion and hiring of government employees is a function of their competencies and performance – i.e. merit-based HRM - governance of the public system is enhanced.

In most public sector pay systems, pay increases with seniority within the same job position. Pay increases with seniority for two main reasons: first, experience increases productivity hence an efficient pay system must reward time spent on a job; second, pay increases with seniority in an "implicit contract". The idea of this implicit contract between the employer and the employees is to pay less when the employee is young and higher when older, in order to keep employees in the job position. By paying them less today but more tomorrow, the employer gives incentives to stay and wait to benefit from the seniority effect. Keeping them in the administration or the firm when they are young is useful when there is a specific human capital to invest in. This specific human capital covers training, competencies, knowledge worthy in the public sector and that may be useless in the private sector or on another job position. If the employee plans to quit the public sector, then it is not worth investing in specific human capital. Consequently, salaries rise more quickly than productivity with seniority, in order to increase the incentives to specific training and to keep young talent.

Today the age-wage profile has become flatter in the private sector but also in the public sector in most OECD member countries, for instance in Japan, Korea but also in the United States and France. One reason is that the rhythm of change in technology makes it more appealing to hire young and competent employees without committing to long-term employment. Another reason might be the weakening of specific human capital for public sector jobs. Training on digital competencies, for instance, will be useful on the job market and not only in the specific institution.

Mobility between the private and the public sector and mobility between firms weakens the implicit contract. Hence, managers can pay according to productivity all along the career and the rate of increase of pay with seniority is expected to be lower.

In Israel, the public sector still gives a high weight to seniority in salary. If the relative pay of older employees to younger employees is higher in the public sector than in the private sector, a shortage of young public employees is to be expected. Even if on average, one finds no pay gap between the public and the private sector, there could be an important misalignment by age. If the private sector follows the implicit contract effect less than the public sector, then younger employees will be paid according to their productivity and not less, hence young employees will be less attracted to the public sector.

For instance in the education sector, the wage gap between young and older teachers in Israel is rather wide compared to other OECD member countries (OECD, 2019[8]). Among the secondary teachers (Figure 2.4), on average an older teacher that reaches the salary at top of scale earns around 2.7 times more than a younger teacher at the starting salary in Israel, whereas the ratio is on average 1.8 across OECD member countries, 2,1 in France, 1.7 in the United stated, 1,3 in Sweden and Germany. This will likely have a negative impact on the number of, and quality of young people who wish to become teachers in the public system. To limit this reduced attractiveness of the public sector for young teachers, in March 2018, a labour agreement was signed by the government, local authorities and the high-school teachers' union that implemented an increase in wages for teachers starting their career by approximately 20%. Those teachers make up about 6% of the teachers in Israel as of 2018.

Figure 2.4. Lower secondary teachers' statutory salaries at different points in teachers' careers (2018)

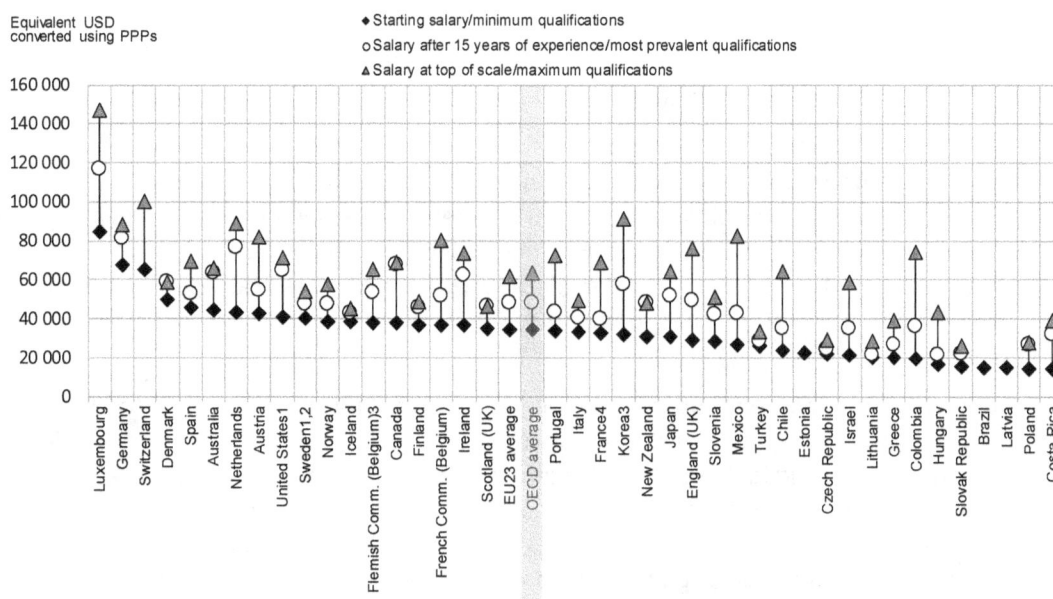

Note: 1. Actual base salaries. 2. Salaries at top of scale and minimum qualifications, instead of maximum qualifications. 3. Salaries at top of scale and most prevalent qualifications, instead of maximum qualifications. 4. Includes the average of fixed bonuses for overtime hours. Countries and economies are ranked in descending order of starting salaries for lower secondary teachers with minimum qualifications.
Source: OECD (2019), Table D3.1a, Tables D3.1c and D3.6, available on line. See Source section for more information and Annex 3 for notes (https://doi.org/10.1787/f8d7880d-en.).

The evolution of salary along the career is linked to the pension system. In Israel, in 2002 a pension reform took place which began a shift from a defined benefit plan to a defined contribution plan. In a defined benefits plan the employer guarantees a retirement benefit amount based on the employee's salary and years of service. A defined contribution plan is funded by the employee who defers a portion of their gross salary, with the employer matching contributions to a certain amount. Israel chose to implement the transition between the two systems by not allowing new employees to be on the defined benefits plan. The number of employees on a defined benefit plan is decreasing over time since the new workers are on a defined contribution plan.

This transition distorts incentives between workers for a pay increase. The new workers on defined contributions pensions save their whole career hence care greatly about their wages when young since early savings offer a greater opportunity to compound over their lifetimes; whereas the old workers on defined benefits plans care more about their wages at the end of their career, since this calculates their retirement benefits. It seems challenging to have workers doing the same job but having different pensions systems and gaps between workers may weaken motivation. Consequently, this pension reform exerts additional pressure on rebalancing pay to provide higher pay early in careers and less later, meaning giving less weight for seniority in pay determination.

To conclude, promotions are an effective tool to reward performance and talent when they are based on assessment of competence and performance, rather than being automatic based on seniority. The importance of seniority in pay is inconsistent with the reform of pensions Israel has implemented and the changes expected in the future of work, and a decreased use of seniority compared to other variables could help in attracting young talents.

OECD Recommendations for a more effective pay system in Israel

In order to improve Israel's public sector pay system and ensure it supports a public service which is forward-looking, flexible and fulfilling to a diverse range of public services, the Israel government could aim to:

1. **Develop a common strategic vision for the future of the public sector in Israel.** This should include a specific focus on which skills and competencies need to be developed and how. This could be done centrally, but also in individual sectors, agencies and ministries. It should be an inclusive activity bringing together the Ministry of Finance, Civil Service Commission, line managers and employees. It can then be used to guide pay reforms and collective bargaining processes.

2. **Reduce the number and specificity of job classifications.** Greater standardisation of positions across the public sector would enable mobility between and across Ministries. Mapping and grouping job types enables targeted interventions to help staff adapt and upskill in a context where digitalisation and other trends are re-shaping work, workforces and workplaces. Revised job classifications that focus on competences is key to embedding greater flexibility, i.e. the understanding that all jobs will and must change their scope.

3. **Align pay more closely with the competencies and complexity demanded in positions.** Building on the recommendation above, linking pay more clearly with the complexity and 'weight' of a job rather than static indicators such as educational background would encourage high performance and attract needed skill sets. This may call for a Job Evaluation exercise

targeting specific professions. This review could be piloted for areas of the public service demonstrating clear evidence of a persistent inability to recruit and retain specialised and high-value skill sets.

4. **Rationalise the structure of pay to increase base pay vis-à-vis additional pay.** Many allowances are no longer linked to the reason they were introduced in the first place. This complexity impedes recruitment and mobility. Other allowances may have unintended side effects, such as creating an expectation of compensation for undertaking training. Reviewing and rationalising certain allowances would help create greater clarity on pay. This could free up funds to be used more strategically, e.g. for targeted pay increases.

5. **Unwind links between and across pay groups.** Currently, the web of collective agreements means that it is difficult to adjust pay in one area without creating knock-on expectations or automatic adjustments in other unrelated areas. While respecting unions' prerogatives to defend their members, there should be greater 'ring-fencing' of the scope of negotiations between the government and unions. This means that negotiations would focus on a clearly defined population, allowing more nuanced adjustments to collective agreements and ultimately, mutual gains.

6. **Establish a list of hard-to-recruit profiles/positions and pilot creative ways to align pay with relevant market levels.** Pay is not the only factor determining why people apply to and remain in the public sector, but it is an important factor. Increasing pay to an acceptable level for specific and high-value positions could be funded from efficiency gains elsewhere to raise base salary, or through performance-related payments based on rigorous criteria.

7. **Decentralise and review pay-for-performance systems.** Israel's dual performance pay systems (group or individual) should be reviewed and rebalanced – focused on better aligning the system with the nature of the work. This will likely result in a number of areas currently under the group regime transitioning to the individual regime, for which managers need a degree of autonomy to allow them to set performance norms and reward high performers, while remaining within an agreed-upon budget ceiling. This discretion should be framed by clear, rigorous and periodically reviewed guidance and support. For groups that remain in the group system, performance metrics should be updated regularly, to ensure continued relevance. The committee system should also be reviewed to ensure they provide managers and employees with the right tools to set effective performance indicators.

8. **Reduce the importance of seniority-based pay.** To be effective as incentives, pay and promotions should be linked with actual performance rather than only static indicators, such as seniority (length in post). Entry-level or starting salaries could be made more attractive in line with an increased emphasis on performance management and merit-based promotions.

9. **Expand the time-bound contract employment model.** Expanding this contractual modality to additional management jobs or to technological positions could be a key driver of greater flexibility and attractiveness. The purpose of this reform was to create a competitive environment for senior employees since these contracts enable higher salaries to be paid for in-demand skills, as well as inducing a higher turnover rate in senior management, therefore creating a more dynamic organisations.

References

Cabinet Office (2020), *Civil Service pay remit guidance 2020/21*, [5]
https://www.gov.uk/government/publications/civil-service-pay-remit-guidance-202021/civil-service-pay-remit-guidance-202021#pay-flexibility.

Gallup (2016), *How Millenials Want to Work and Live*, [3]
https://www.gallup.com/workplace/238073/millennials-work-live.aspx.

Mazar, Y. (2018), "Differences in Skill Levels of Educated Workers Between the Public and [1]
private Sectors, the Return to Skills and the Connection between them: Evidence from the
PIAAC Surveys", *Bank of Israel Working Papers*, Vol. 2018/1, pp. 1-28,
https://www.boi.org.il/en/Research/DiscussionPapers1/dp201801e.pdf.

OECD (2019), *Education at a Glance 2019: OECD Indicators*, OECD Publishing, Paris, [8]
https://dx.doi.org/10.1787/f8d7880d-en.

OECD (2018), *Policy brief on the Future of Work: Putting faces to the jobs at risk of automation*, [2]
https://www.oecd.org/employment/Automation-policy-brief-2018.pdf.

OECD (2005), *Performance-related Pay Policies for Government Employees*, OECD Publishing, [7]
Paris, https://dx.doi.org/10.1787/9789264007550-en.

Postel-Vinay, F. and H. Turon (2007), *The Public Pay Gap in Britain: Small Differences That* [4]
(Don't?) Matter, https://doi.org/10.1111/j.1468-0297.2007.02091.x.

Wenzel, A., T. Krause and D. Vogel (2017), *Making Performance Pay Work: The Impact of* [6]
Transparency, Participation, and Fairness on Controlling Perception and Intrinsic Motivation,
https://doi.org/10.1177%2F0734371X17715502.

3 Improving Labour Relations in Israel's Public Sector

This chapter discusses labour relations in Israel's public sector. It focuses on the institutions and actors involved in collective bargaining, as well as the dynamics of labour disputes. It draws on international examples of good practice to discuss the benefits and challenges of centralising negotiations in the Ministry of Finance, protecting essential services from strike actions, and establishing effective alternative dispute resolution structures. The chapter concludes with recommendations for reforms to the legal framework and general approach to collective bargaining.

In Israel, the main frameworks governing labour relations were designed in the 1950s and provide a significant degree of strength to public sector unions. Today, the world of work and social expectations are changing at increasingly fast pace, and there is an urgent need to rebuild social dialogue and improve labour relations so that the Israeli public service can implement reforms necessary to keep pace. In 2007, Cohen et al (2007[1]), observed that, "the prevailing political climate has led to the popular argument that Israeli trade unions have always been, and continue to be, extremely militant in their strategies and inconsiderate of economic constraints". Today, this view still holds among many observers and public managers, who feel that unions have a disproportionate amount of influence in management affairs in the public sector, in part due to a legal regime which is no longer fit-for-purpose. On the other hand, union representatives feel aggrieved at what they perceive to be far-reaching changes to their members' working conditions not being reasonably compensated.

In Israel, unions have the possibility to disrupt a wide range of management-driven modernisation reforms including the introduction of new technologies that reshape work tasks, the implementation of mobility reforms that aim to make the workforce more flexible, and any reconsideration of the pay system recommendations of the previous chapter. Therefore, unions have to be engaged as key partners and social dialogue has to be improved to create the forum needed to agree to a common vision of the future of public employment in Israel's public sector. The OECD's 2018 Jobs Strategy shows that wage-setting institutions can contribute to a broader sharing of productivity benefits without undermining employment or the basis for productivity itself (OECD, 2018[2]). To do this, there needs to be good will and trust on both sides, and a legal framework that provides an even playing field in terms of what is negotiated, when and by whom.

A recent report by the OECD shows how collective bargaining helps support challenges faced by the future of work. It shows that, "Providing that institutions are well designed, collective bargaining systems can help employers and unions find mutually beneficial solutions and establish a level-playing field for all companies and workers. However, fruitful exchanges between social partners are not a given and collective bargaining systems need to strike a balance between inclusiveness and flexibility (OECD, 2019[3])."

The challenge for Israel's public sector is to re-establish that balance between inclusiveness and flexibility and reconsider the institutions needed. However, social dialogue in Israel's public sector seems to be stuck, resorting too often to strike action. Talks between public employers and unions appear to occur primarily when there is a crisis or problem, which impedes information-sharing and the building of trust. Israel must find a way to re-build sound and inclusive social dialogue in order to improve public service delivery because there can be no effective public service without trust and collaboration of all stakeholders including employees.

Collective bargaining in the public sector

Public sector bargaining has evolved through four stages in many OECD member countries, in Europe and the United Stated in particular: the expansionary years (mid-1960s to 1982) where it benefitted from growth and laws that allowed for collective bargaining in the public sector; the restraint years (1982-1990) where it went under attack, the retrenchment years (1990s) marked by restructuring and downsizing, and the consolidation years (after 1998) marked by economic expansion, the restoration of fiscal stability and increases in public employment. Public sector unions also increased memberships and negotiated increases in wages (OECD, 2019[4]). With the economic crisis, a new period started characterized by cuts or freezes in employment and wages, which is a challenge to social dialogue.

The situation of Israel contrasts to this history of labour relations. The most recent period is not characterized by budget cuts or pay freeze but rather resembles the restraint years of the 1980s: strong labour disputes; high levels of distrust between unions and the executive, high resistance to reform, and the idea that a path to reforms requires weakening the unions. Most of the OECD member countries that went through this tense period came to find that unions could be collaborative social partners who allow reforms to be socially accepted and effective.

Since the 2008 global financial crisis, reforms in many OECD countries were aimed at strengthening firm-level bargaining and giving more flexibility to employers in case of economic shocks (Box 3.1) but were, in some cases, partly revised in recent years, to emphasise greater coordination between national-level and firm-level actors. The challenges posed by the Covid-19 pandemic may give rise to further pressure to reform labour relations: trade-offs may become more acute in times of health and economic crisis as the government seeks to ensure continuity of service and the safety of public sector workers. As such, the challenge facing Israel is to design a reform of labour relations without undermining trust and motivation and avoiding restructuring or downsizing if possible.

Box 3.1. The reforms of collective bargaining during the global financial crisis

Spain, Portugal, Greece and France passed encompassing labour market reforms during or following the crisis that also changed the way collective bargaining works.

In Greece, the collective bargaining system was completely overhauled during the crisis. The favourability principle was suspended giving priority to firm-level agreements. Moreover, new provisions allowed "associations of persons" (i.e. association of workers, not necessarily affiliated to a union) to sign firm-level agreements on top of trade unions. Extensions of collective agreements to non-signatory firms were also suspended and limits to the duration and the ultra-activity of collective agreements were introduced. Finally, the system of unilateral recourse to arbitration was abolished. Since Greece exited the European Stability Mechanism stability support programme (i.e. the financial support programme set up during the crisis) in September 2018, the favourability principle and the possibility of extending sectoral collective agreements signed by representative parties have been re-introduced. Since September 2018, 12 sectoral or local collective agreements have been extended, covering in total more than 200 000 workers. The unilateral recourse to arbitration has also been re-instated by a Council of State ruling in 2014 but some incentives for a consensual solution have been introduced. The new Greek Government elected in June 2019 has expressed the intention to again limit unilateral appeals to arbitration and the use of extensions as well as to introduce opt-out mechanisms from sectoral agreements.

In Spain, the 2012 reform inverted the favourability principle giving priority to firm-level agreements over those at sectoral or regional level. The reform also made it easier for firms to opt-out from higher-level agreements or firm-level agreements either upon an agreement with worker representatives or by unilaterally referring the matter to arbitration by a public tripartite body. For the time being, Spanish firms do not appear to have made a significant use of these new provisions.

In Portugal, successive reforms between 2011 and 2015 initially froze extensions of collective agreements and then granted them only if the signing employer organisations met certain criteria. The duration and ultra-activity of collective agreements was reduced. Works councils in firms with at least 150 employees (down from 500) were allowed to negotiate firm-level agreements upon a mandate from unions and a possibility was introduced for employers to temporarily suspend a collective agreement in case of crisis. Since 2015, these reforms have been partly reversed: in 2017 a tripartite pact removed the representativeness criteria for extensions and set a limit of 35 days for their issuance to avoid the usual and long pre-reform delays. Limits to ultra-activity were suspended for 18 months between 2017 and 2018 to create stability for negotiating a tripartite agreement to amend the Labour Code. Sectoral bargaining has now resumed. By contrast, despite the new provisions that are still valid, there has been a very limited take-up on the possibility to negotiate at company level.

In France, two main reforms took place in the recent years. In 2016, the Labour Law (Loi El Khomri) strengthened the role of firm-level agreements in defining working time, leave and rest period. It also increased the threshold to define which trade unions are representative and allowed to sign firm-level agreements and introduced the possibility of approving the agreements via an internal referendum. Opt-out clauses in case of economic difficulties, with the objective of safeguarding employment have also been introduced (but not on wages). In 2018 the Law ratifying the September 2017 Ordonnances went further to promote firm-level bargaining by allowing negotiations even in the absence of a union in firms with less than 50 employees. Moreover, in companies with less than 20 employees the employer can submit a proposal of agreement directly to an internal referendum. The reform also sought to make extensions of sectoral agreements less automatic by conditioning them to the presence of different provisions by firm size and by introducing the possibility to block them out of public interest considerations (in particular, if an agreement is used as an anticompetitive tool against non-signatory companies) based on the evaluation of an ad hoc experts group. Two years after the Ordonnances, however, no request of extension has been refused and no agreement has included different provisions for large and small firms. The Ordonnances reform also merged and streamlined different firm-level workers' representation bodies into a single one with the goal to simplify dialogue at firm level.

Source: OECD (2019), Negotiating Our Way Up: Collective Bargaining in a Changing World of Work, OECD Publishing, Paris, https://doi.org/10.1787/1fd2da34-en.

Dynamics of social dialogue in the public sector

When it comes to labour relations, the state is both a legislator and employer. Hence, collective bargaining in the public sector is not the same as in the private sector, and must be understood *vis-à-vis* the authority of the government.

This includes the authority to establish public budgets which determine and allocate public spending. In the private sector there is a real affordability constraint on collective bargaining, as it is in no unions' interest to negotiate an unsustainable salary level that threatens to put the firm out of business and leave members jobless. However, in the public sector, this constraint is less natural, since governments have options to fund pay increases through increased taxes, deficit spending/borrowing or internal reallocation. Given that compensation of public employees accounts for above 20% of public spending on average in OECD countries (and above 26% in Israel), unions can have a significant impact on the public budget.

Without an affordability constraint, there is no direct trade-off between the number of jobs and the level of pay: when unions negotiate wage gains it doesn't directly threaten their jobs since this wage increase could be paid by taxpayers. On the contrary in the private sector, there is a trade-off between wage increases and the number of jobs and unions can accept a wage freeze if the number of jobs is increased or even sustained.

Other arguments have often accompanied some reluctance to give public employees the same bargaining rights as private employees. These include arguments that public sector unions could exploit a power in negotiation due to the fact that they can rarely be fired. The right to strike could be regarded as undermining essential service delivery, and they have a monopolistic power in delivering essential public services. Therefore, strike actions in the public sector can result in significant impacts felt by the population at large, rather than private owners or shareholders of a business, as is typically the case in the private sector.

However, in public services, even if there is no market constraint, there is a user constraint: students, patients or users of public services exert pressure on public employees not to strike or act detrimentally.

The suggests that public perception exerts limits on what a trade union in the public sector can do. For example, teachers' strikes which are not appropriately justified in the public sphere can give the impression that teachers' unions are punishing children and families, thereby reducing the power of unions at the negotiation table. However, this constraint can cut both ways, since politicians and management may be willing to avoid strikes at high costs in order to maintain a positive public image, particularly at key political moments.

Job stability in the public sector may also enable stability of union membership, hence the stability of the actors of collective bargaining. Union members have a higher power in the negotiations as they usually remain in the public institutions longer than the politicians who represent the government. This job stability both increases the union's knowledge of needed reforms and can be a leverage to consider them as social partner for growth. However it also gives power to resist change.

Many labour economists such as Richard Freeman challenged the idea that unions may be detrimental to productivity and showed that unions increase employees' morale and motivation, hence productivity. Unions can enhance on-the-job training and diminish turnover. Workplace innovations depend on meaningful union participation. Unions can induce lower quit rates, better job production standards, more information exchange and better communications. Although there is evidence of this positive effect in the private sector, there are a few studies in the public sector (OECD, 2019[5]), (OECD, 2019[6])). For instance (OECD, 2019[7]), find that on average students are seven percent more productive in unionised schools. On the contrary, (OECD, 2019[8]) finds that teachers' unions have a negative overall effect on student performance, even though they tend to have a positive impact on schools' resources, because of a detrimental effect on productivity.

Box 3.2. Collective bargaining in the private sector, worker 'voice', and performance: selected findings from "Negotiating Our Way Up: Collective Bargaining in a Changing World of Work"

- Wage coordination is a key tool to help the social partners account for the business-cycle situation and the macroeconomic effects of wage agreements on competitiveness. Co-ordinated bargaining systems are linked with higher employment and lower unemployment (including for young people, women and low-skilled workers) than systems where bargaining happens only at firm level.

- Bargaining systems that leave little scope for firms to tailor the conditions set in higher-level agreements tend to be associated with lower productivity growth, if coverage of agreements is high. This result suggests that the lack of flexibility at firm level, which characterises centralised bargaining systems, may come at the expense of lower productivity growth

- Best outcomes in terms of employment, productivity and wages seem to be reached when sectoral agreements set broad framework conditions but leave detailed provisions to firm-level negotiations.

- The main challenge for social partners and governments is to adjust collective bargaining systems to achieve better outcomes in terms of employment, job quality and inclusiveness, while leaving scope for firms to adapt agreements to their own situations.

- Both direct and "mixed" forms of voice (where workers' representatives coexist with direct dialogue between workers and managers) are associated with a higher quality of the working environment (compared with the absence of voice). By contrast, the presence of workers'

> representatives in firms where there are no parallel means of direct exchange between workers and managers is not associated with a better quality of the working environment.
>
> Source: OECD (2019), Negotiating Our Way Up: Collective Bargaining in a Changing World of Work, OECD Publishing, Paris, https://doi.org/10.1787/1fd2da34-en.

Who negotiates, on what, and when

There are preliminary questions to answer before entering a negotiation: who negotiates on behalf of whom, at which frequency, on what topics and how binding are those negotiations? This section looks at these aspects of the legal and institutional frameworks that govern and manage labour relations in Israel. It shows that striking an ideal balance across these three factors requires changes to the legal frameworks and to the institutional actors and mindsets that have become embedded in the public sector.

Who: centralised negotiations

In Israel, there are not many unions but they are partly decentralized – regardless of their appearance. For instance, in the education sector (there are 200,000 teachers in the Israeli education system, most, 130,000, directly employed by the Ministry of Education), there are two unions who do not always agree or speak with the same voice. In the security sector, police officers and the military cannot unionise, but are impacted directly by other unions: there is a direct link (through law or executive order) between what civil servants negotiate and what the military receives so when one union obtains a gain it benefits many sectors, even the non-unionized ones. (It is also worth noting that these non-unionised entities are well organised through e.g. veterans organisations). The unionisation rate is rather high and increasing in recent years, which contrasts with the situation of other OECD member countries. Unions can be partially funded by public funds, even if they mainly rely on their own funds. Again, this situation differs from other OECD member countries where unions for more than two-thirds of OECD countries rely exclusively on their own funds.

In Israel, the role of unions extends beyond pay negotiations, to also include direct employee support. There seems to be a common perception that when workers have an issue with their managers, their working environment, pay, or anything related to work, they go to the unions rather than raising issues directly with management through, e.g. councillors or mediators.

On the government side, the Ministry of Finance represents the government on all matters; it supervises and authorises all agreements, and often defines the strategy and leads the negotiations. Negotiations for the whole public sector employment framework are centralized in the Ministry of Finance. Hence, centralization is a prominent feature of the negotiation process.

There are pros and cons to centralisation of negotiations. The economics literature demonstrates the relative efficiency of centralized bargaining. This is because wage bargaining creates not only direct effects on the employees and firms engaged in the negotiation, but also indirect effects on the whole labour market. Those external effects are better taken into account in centralized bargaining. For instance, a wage increase in a municipality can attract workers from outside, hence creating a negative effect on the other neighbouring towns. A local wage increase can also create a second effect on the neighbouring towns; an "envy" externality that could make other employees not covered by the agreement dissatisfied, reducing their well-being and motivation. All those impacts of local negotiations on other administrations are better handled in a centralized bargaining process.

One of the main arguments for Israel's level of centralisation is to avoid situations where benefits awarded by one ministry in a specific context become expected by all in every context. Collective agreements

(Collective Agreements Law of 1957) are linked either through an index or one to the other. Any agreement in one sector has various effects on the other ministries. Hence when negotiating, the government needs to anticipate what would happen if one single agreement changes. Coordination is led by the Ministry of Finance's Wages and Labour Agreements Division.

There is also a learning curve in negotiations, and a centralized body gains comparative advantage in dealing with arbitration, labour contracts and labour disputes. Therefore, centralisation of negotiation in the Ministry of Finance may be necessary to avoid situations where decentralized negotiations fall into the hands of managers who are less competent at negotiating. As discussed in chapter 1, line managers' loyalties are not always in line with the management function. Decentralisation of negotiation is effective only if senior officers are professional, incentivized managers who can enter into constructive negotiations with their employees. This would also require that managers not be covered by the same collective agreements as their employees – and this is not always the case in Israel's public sector.

However, centralization of bargaining is not optimal if it weakens the managers' incentives and autonomy. Many OECD countries have experienced decentralization of bargaining to ministries and agencies mainly because decentralization gives managers the ability and incentive to design employment and pay systems that match their business needs, and control and reward performance. Decentralization goes with individualized management of competencies and performance management, since employment systems are an important tool to achieve organisational performance objectives. Decentralisation can also be a way of introducing an affordability constraint and maintaining the integrity of the overall budget, since broad allocations are not up for negotiation, and therefore the negotiation focuses on how best to distribute the allocated wage bill and how to find internal efficiencies that could supplement it.

High levels of centralisation may also reduce managers' abilities and willingness to negotiate for reforms that are not directly related to pay, but which impact the public service. For example, in many OECD countries, reforms such as the introduction of new technology, changes to the performance assessment systems, or improvements to job classification, can be written into collective agreements, so that pay increases are traded for reforms in areas that make public employment more flexible. In Israel, these kinds of negotiations have also been effective, for example, when negotiations with local government employees enabled the introduction of new technologies. However, since the institutions responsible for these reforms are not within the ministry of Finance there is a risk that these strategic opportunities are not fully leveraged or understood when negotiations are centralised in one unit.

In most OECD countries, decentralisation does not affect equally all the topics that are negotiated. Collective bargaining at the central level often relates to base salary, overall wage expenditure or global working conditions. On the contrary, negotiations are decentralized when it comes to new management tools and performance pay. Sweden is an example of decentralization embedded in a centralized bargain process that takes the best from both systems (see Box 3.3 for the example of decentralization of negotiations in Sweden and the UK). Decentralisation of pay, as in Sweden and the UK, means that managers have greater discretion to use their budget to reward high performers and attract specific profiles. Managers also have scope to trade different elements according to needs, e.g. by offering higher pay for fewer workers (or vice-versa). Additionally, both managers and unions know what the upper limit of their bargaining wage increases are, as they are set in budget allocations or framework agreements, creating an affordability constraint at the lower level (see more on this below).

Regardless of the level of centralisation in Israel, line managers in ministries should be more involved in wage negotiations. For instance in health, it could be useful to take into consideration all the sectoral specificities and try to make the Ministry of Health much more engaged in the resolution of labour issues. In Israel, the equilibrium between the two ministries, the Ministry of Finance and the Ministry of Health, seems to be shifting and the latter with more decentralised responsibility over budgets, wages, and numbers of positions. Their power of negotiation with public employees, i.e. doctors, is stronger than in other sectors, and this example could serve as a standard for future decentralization of negotiations.

The Civil Service Commission (CSC) is another strategic partners for collective bargaining when negotiations are focused on the employees of the central governments employed by the CSC. The CSC accompanies government ministries in managing labor disputes as part of its role as a regulator and professional knowledge center on human capital management issues. The CSC can represent the state employer's point of view at the discussion table, and bring a broad view regarding human capital management. Since the CSC as an employer and regulator has special expertise in the field of human capital, the CSC can help to increase management capacity by establishing trust between management and employees, and increase the ability to implement agreements. Working together with the Ministry of Finance helps to streamline the process for the state as an employer, and enable more forward-looking solutions that take into account the full employment relationship. Partnership and coordination between the two units is important, as the management of the human capital at the Ministries and economic considerations are intertwined.

Box 3.3. Decentralisation of public sector bargaining in Sweden and the UK

Sweden's resilience to the economic crisis of 2008 can be explained in part by the developed sound system of social dialogue and active involvement of social partners (see (OECD, 2019[9])). The Swedish bargaining system is a centralized two-tier system: firstly, bargaining takes place at the sectoral level and afterward at the organization level and there has been a clear tendency to the decentralization of wage determination and other topics at the organization level.

Swedish public employees are subject to the same labour market regulations as private employees. Hence, all employees have legally guaranteed rights to bargaining and industrial actions. There is one labour law for all (except very specific cases as judges).

SAGE (Arbetgivarverket), the Swedish agency for government employers, counts 250 member agencies and 240,000 employees in the central government sector. At the local government level, the employer organization is the Swedish Association of Local Authorities and Regions (SALAR, Sveriges Kommuner och Regioner, SKR) representing 290 municipalities and 20 regions.

Due to a high level of social conflicts in the Swedish labour market, a central national agreement was established in 1938 to support the value of collective agreements for both employers and employees. The agreement stated that social conflicts were not allowed during the binding period of collective agreements on national or sectoral level. In 1974, this regulation was included in Sweden's labour market legislation.

An "Industry Agreement" on Cooperation on Industrial Development and Salary Formation, established in 1997, is still in force. It is the basis for salary revisions in the Swedish labour markets. The agreement states that salary negotiations should start in the industry sector since that sector is involved in international competition. The other sectoral agreements should be negotiated after, and using the industry agreement as a benchmark. This harmonization has made the period of salary negotiations much more peaceful with almost no social conflicts. Social agreements are binding but there is no need for legal acts. Agreements complement the labour market law, such as pension agreements and job security agreements.

In **the UK**, in line with the delegated pay framework, negotiation with trade unions on pay takes place at departmental [Ministry] level. Departments are encouraged to work constructively with trade unions on the development of their overall pay and reward strategies. Departments should also work constructively with trade unions for pay purposes, for both annual pay remits and the development of pay flexibility business cases. Departments may enter into formal negotiations with trade unions once their remit has been agreed by the relevant Secretary of State.

When it works well, decentralised bargaining can result in win-win-win deals through collective agreement. In its best form, the organisation – in this case each Department – evaluates workforce reforms to improve efficiency, productivity and improvements in public service. This can be a blend of abolishing outdated payments and practices, longer and more flexible working arrangements for the workforce, etc. The savings identified from these improvements are offered as "gain sharing" arrangements to unions/employees as higher pay which will be given if collective agreement is reached to the reform of contracts, terms and conditions and working arrangements. The end result is a more transparent pay system, better retention and recruitment of skilled workers, improved public services and more motivated employees and better labour relations. This is not a straightforward process and requires time and skill to design deals well that work for all three participants (unions/employees, public/finance/treasury and Organisations).

Towards an affordability constraint

Most OECD countries have found ways of creating a necessary distance between the budget domain and the collective bargaining domain. This is necessary to create clarity of "what is on the table" and safeguard the democratic right of elected governments to allocate public spending based on their political priorities. This is often done through decentralisation whereby ministries or agencies are given "lump sum" appropriations. An affordability constraint, implemented at individual Ministry or agency level can provide greater transparency to unions on what is available for negotiations, and limit spill-over effects on other parts of the public sector. Another option is to create affordability constraints by separating the budgeting and labour functions through the creation of separate negotiating agencies. For example, in Canada, where negotiations are centralised, the Treasury Board Secretariat, not the Department of Finance, is the employer and manages all the wage negotiations. A third option is to set the affordability constraints in national framework agreements, taking into consideration macro-economic data, and to use that agreement to constrain local-level agreements accordingly.

In Israel, both wage negotiations and budgeting are conducted by the Ministry of Finance, although wage negotiations are overseen by a separate Public Sector Wages and Labour Agreements Division, and this provides an important level of separation between the two functions. Today, the Budget Division is not actively present in negotiations that do not include structural changes and reforms. Occasionally, the Budget Division agrees in advance with the Wages and Labour Agreements Division the boundaries of the budget for each deal and does not sit at the negotiating table. This is an important separation and one that can help to ensure an affordability constraint. However, there could be opportunities to further strengthen the constraint through gradual decentralisation and/or additional separation between the budgeting and wage negotiation functions. In any event, macroeconomic indicators could be used in the bargaining process as a way to constrain negotiations. An independent third party could prepare this analysis, which could help to inform framework agreements, which, in turn, could set upper limits for local-level agreements.

Eventually, the effective level of centralisation depends on the quality and strength of social dialogue. In the present state of social dialogue in Israel, decentralisation cannot be effective if not linked to a major reform in the legal framework that governs labour relations, as it will be argued in the following section. Managers and heads of public entities (ministries, agencies, etc.) might find it convenient to leave negotiations to the centralized level that is perceived as able to both resist a labour dispute and rule over budget expenses.

What is negotiated: a wide range of working conditions

The topics covered by negotiations in OECD countries are wide-ranging. In Israel, there is a broad definition of working conditions and the unions are entitled to demand negotiations or strike due to the consequences of any changes in the working conditions. Practically this means that any minor change must be accepted by the employees including a change in the location, the scope of work or the tools used. Unions use their power to include in wage agreements a set of detailed issues. Hence, unions are involved in nearly any small change in the working conditions, and all topics are covered by the same institutional organisation.

Compared to other OECD member countries, the importance of negotiation with unions seems to be more prominent in many areas in Israel (Figure 3.1). In Israel, agreement with unions is "mandatory" regarding base salary and social benefits, additional pay or performance pay. Unions must also be consulted in reforms regarding the employment framework, the right to strike, management tools or government structuring and working conditions. In practice, there is no precise definition of working conditions which means that unions expect to be consulted on all topics, and retain the right to strike whenever they disagree.

Figure 3.1. Involvement of unions in specific issues

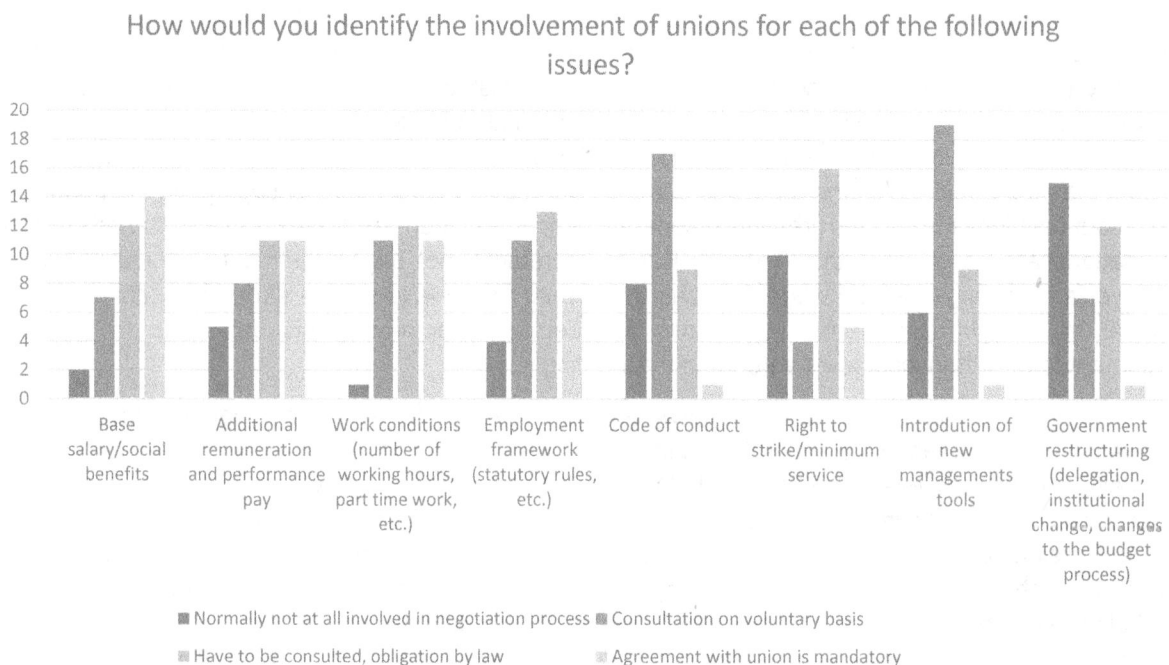

How would you identify the involvement of unions for each of the following issues?

Source: OECD (2020), Survey of members of the OECD Working Party on Public Employment and Management

An additional factor to consider is the question of the protection of essential services. Most OECD countries designate some public services as essential in order to reduce the exposure of vulnerable citizens to work stoppages. Indeed, one needs to find the right balance between the rights of public employees to strike and the well-being of the general population. The definition and scope of what is considered to be an "essential service" varies. It depends on the country and its particular circumstances. The criterion used to designate a service as "essential", recommended by the ILO, is "the existence of a clear and imminent threat to the life, personal safety or health of the whole or part of the population." Services designated as essential may still negotiate for the same range of factors as others, but are limited in their ability to strike. The use of binding arbitration is often greater. In Israel, only the security services are limited in this regard. Given the recent experience in designating essential services in the context of the pandemic crisis, Israel may wish to launch a discussion on this topic amongst within the government and among the relevant social partners.

Box 3.4. Essential services and the right to strike

In Italy, essential public services are defined by law and include health, civil protection, justice, waste services, energy, education, transport, postal services and telecommunication services. In the UK, there is no definition of essential services, but the Trade Union Act of 2016 considers that in "important public service", industrial actions require the support of 40% of the workforce in health, education, fire services, transport, nuclear installations and border security. In France there is no precise definition of essential services and no general restrictions on strike for essential services. However, in order to limit the cost of strikes in terms of public service delivery, France like other countries have regulated the right to strike in order to ensure minimum public service delivery.

In many other OECD member countries, some limitations to the right of strike are implemented in order to maintain those essential services. For instance, if agreements cannot be reached, alternative dispute resolution mechanisms such as binding arbitration can be used in these areas. The International Labor Organization states that "The imposition of compulsory arbitration in cases in which the parties do not reach an agreement [...] is admissible". In Spain, for instance, the government may decide on the resumption of work activities when there is a threat or a "serious damage" resulting for a strike.

When to negotiate: timing of negotiations and strike action

In Israel, there is no predefined timing for labour relations: negotiations and industrial actions may begin before, last during and linger on after the agreements. Moreover, there is no specific timing for negotiation; it could occur at any time, at the best opportunistic moment, and often under the stress of a strike. Moreover, the signing of a collective agreement, even when it includes articles governing industrial peace for a defined moment in time, does not completely preclude employees from participating in work stoppages under certain conditions:

> [T]he obligation for industrial peace does not derogate from the rights of Employees to participate in a work stoppage by law according to labour law principles, announced by the Histadrut on a national level, including regarding the framework or occupational agreement, and this without derogating from the claims of any side regarding work stoppages as described above. (source – Collective Agreement between the Israel Government and the Histadrut Ha'Ovdim Ha'Clalit Ha'Hadasha, 28 April 2015)

Israel may want to move toward a system where the timing of negotiations is predefined and where a concluded agreement must last for a minimum period of time before it can be reopened. Moreover, negotiations can't be everlasting and need to find an exit. In Sweden for instance (Box 3.3), there is a legal obligation to maintain peaceful labour relations throughout the period covered by the agreement. This could be a path to follow for Israel. When social dialogue is built on trust, negotiations don't take place during the time of the agreement but only at a predefined moment between agreements.

Furthermore, in Israel the rules around the timing of strikes could be reviewed. In order to strike, unions register a labour dispute and are then required to wait 14 days before taking industrial action. However there is no expiration date to the labour dispute, suggesting that strikes can take place with no notice once the 14 days has passed. This, and the lack of peace clauses to prevent industrial action, creates a situation where unions can keep open disputes for many months or even years, and have the ability to launch a strike at any opportune moment. For example, a dispute opened by the teachers' union in April, may lay dormant with no negotiation until days before the opening of the school year, at which time the union threatens an immediate strike unless demands are met.

Many countries have more specific rules about when and how strikes can be triggered. In the UK, for example, employees must vote to go on strike for a specific reason and secondary picketing is forbidden. Trade union members have to gain both majority participation and the majority in favour of a strike. Employees on illegal strikes can be dismissed.

To conclude, it is very important to know who the actors of negotiations are and how they are representative of the workforce (see Box 3.5 for a French example of recent reforms to clarify this question). There are pros and cons to the centralized system in Israel. In most OECD member countries a decentralized power of negotiation helps match the needs for change and the demands of the unions. A centralisation of wage negotiations helps to reduce externalities, there are likely ways to decentralise some aspects related to local and marginal topics to improve efficiency. Centralized bargaining could be limited to base wage increase and pay system.

However, for this decentralization to be feasible there is a need for a legal framework which helps create the conditions, timing, and scope for a balanced negotiation. A regular and fixed timing helps stabilise expectations and resolve disputes. The time for negotiations needs to be given in advance to all stakeholders so that unions and employees improve their expectation and public services are not disrupted by those negotiations. Peaceful labour relations should be kept during an agreement, unless one party has clearly violated that agreement and refuses to address that violation. The issues of negotiations need also to be clarified, major issues could be centralized but precise working conditions are better fixed at the decentralized level.

Box 3.5. Renewing social dialogue in France's career based system

Unions need to be representative of the workforce in order to be legitimate. The issue of deciding who participates in negotiations is then very important and needs to be renewed frequently through elections of the workforce and institutional reforms. In 2008, the process of collective bargaining in the public sector was changed by "*les accords de Bercy*" and the subsequent 2010 law (loi n° 2010-751 du 5 juillet 2010 relative à la rénovation du dialogue social) which provided a new legal framework for collective agreements. This had an impact on which unions could officially represent France's large civil service (over 5 million employees)

Before the reforms, there were five main union confederations which were considered "representative", and could sign collective agreements, although there were no specific criteria to define or demonstrate the concept of representation. In 2008, the reforms introduced new criteria to determine whether a union was "representative", based on the results of elections within the workplace for local representation. To be considered as representative in the private sector, a union had to receive at least 8% of the vote at the sector level and national level. In the public sector the bar is lower, at 3% (the result of changes made earlier in 1996).

In the public sector, collective bargaining is still not binding: only law can alter the status of civil servants. The 2010 law gave a formal aspect to negotiations and added the following elements to the negotiating table, which had previously been focused mostly on pay: working conditions, careers and promotions, training, social security, disability, gender inequalities, hygiene, and health at work.

Labour disputes and social dialogue

Social dialogue is a pillar of public institutions and includes first exchange of information between parties, then consultation, negotiations, and eventually collective bargaining or more formal agreements. When labour relations are inclusive and sound, exchange of information and consultation are usually conducive to collective bargaining and formal agreement. However, social partners can be tempted to reduce the cost of social dialogue and erode the first steps, thereby substituting collective bargaining to consultation. In Israel, social partners seem to focus on the formal agreements. Unions seem to be active actors in formal collective bargaining processes whereas it would be efficient and inclusive to consider them as collaborative social partners. With emerging technologies, social partners can help anticipate skills needs. In a majority of OECD member countries, trade unions are involved in skills assessment, strategic planning and training programs (OECD, 2019[10])

One can also note that while collective bargaining is usually legally defined and formal, other forms of social dialogue are more vague and implicit hence more difficult to measure and use in international comparisons. Although the social dialogue is a pillar of public institutions in most OECD member countries, there is a high level of variation across countries, because labour relations are deeply rooted in the country's history, tradition and culture (Bordogna and Pedersini, 2013[11]), as in Israel, where the Histradut played a key role in the political and economic construction of the country.

Disputes are a symptom that labour relations have partially failed. The political objective of all parties including the government is usually not dispute resolution but dispute prevention. Labour disputes are a costly way of reaching an agreement. An efficient and inclusive labour relations framework includes paths for discussion, negotiations, and common agreement.

In Israel, labour disputes seem to have become the normal way of reaching an agreement. The recent resurgence of unionizing activity and the conflicting labour relations has become an urgent issue to tackle in order to restore more harmonious relations and insure inclusive growth in Israel. It is crucial to set a sound base and framework for negotiations. When negotiations fail, employees can resort to industrial actions that can be disruptive and costly for themselves, for the organisation in which they work, for the citizens they serve, and for the whole economy. In Israel, the number of disputes and strikes, and their cost in terms of lost working days are very high, compared to other OECD member countries.

International comparison on labour disputes and in particular on strikes at the country level is very difficult because of the lack of data and differences in definitions and measurement: small work stoppages and partial strikes are sometimes excluded, the public sector is not always accounted for, unauthorized strikes are sometimes included but not always, etc. The main indicator published by the OECD is the ratio of the number of working days lost because of strikes to total working days, for both the public and the private sector (see Figure 3.2).

Figure 3.2. Annual averages of work days lost per 1 000 salaried employees

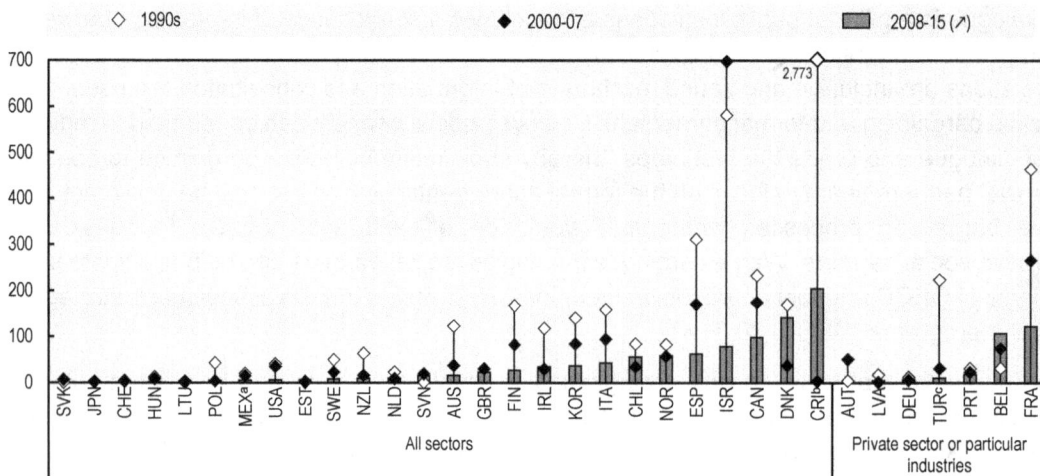

Source: OECD Employment Outlook 2017, Éditions OCDE, Paris, https://doi.org/10.1787/empl_outlook-2017-graph49-en.

To complement these data, the OECD carried out a targeted benchmark survey of Member countries to better understand the legal framework governing sources of strike action (Figure 3.3). The data show that increasing wages is a common reason for industrial action, but also point to changes in contractual relations as a potential source of discord. This figure also shows that other reasons for Industrial action which appear to be commonplace in Israel are either very rare, or illegal in many other OECD countries.

Figure 3.3. Reasons for strike action in the public sector

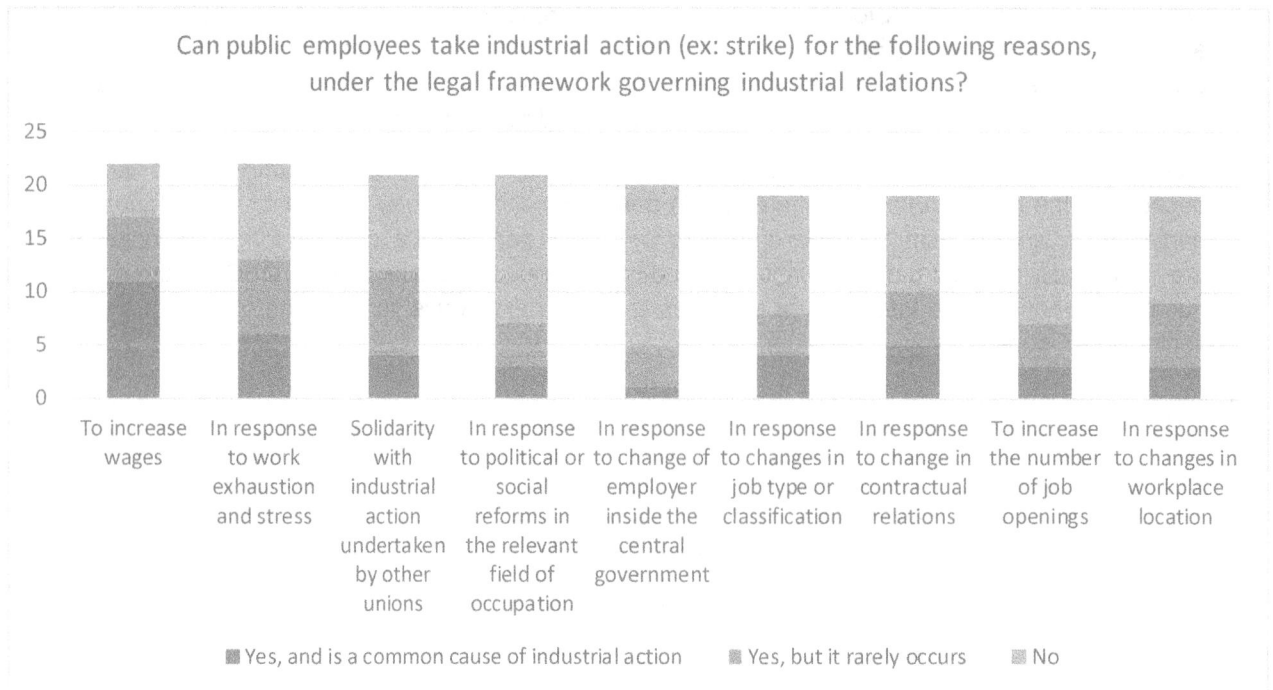

Note: Response based on data provided by 29 out of 37 OECD members. Data were not available for Chile, Estonia, Iceland, Lithuania, Turkey, United States. Colombia is a Member of the OECD but ratified its instrument of Accession to the OECD in April 2020 after the launch of the poll.
Source: OECD poll of PEM Working Party Delegates, January 2020

In the last twenty years, and contrary to the trend in other OECD member countries, one can observe a large numbers of strikers and working days lost as a result of strikes in Israel. This surge can be explained by the strategy to use general strikes in the public sector as a negotiation tool. Unprecedented long-term strikes have also increased the number of days lost and make it necessary to find a path for conflict resolution. In 2018 in Israel, there were 46 different strikes which involved 42000 employees and cost 150 000 days or work. In 2017 the numbers were even higher, when 48 different strikes involved 815 000 employees and cost 672 000 days of work. The large majority of these strikes took place in the public sector.

If long and costly strikes are seen by both employees and unions as the only way to get what they want from negotiations, then Israel would benefit by building institutions that improve social dialogue and negotiations to prevent strikes or other industrial actions. Cohen et al. point to the "total elimination of any alternative methods of dispute resolution in the public sector" as reasons for recourse to strike action (Cohen et al., 2007[1]). This is considered next.

Towards a sound legal framework to settle disputes

Strikes are costly in terms of days of work and it would be more efficient to come to a resolution quickly. After the conflict resolution, one can wonder why a solution that has been rejected at the beginning of the negotiations is eventually accepted by both parties. However, conflict resolutions take time, mainly because time allows for the sharing of information in both directions, and that information is crucial for social dialogue and conflict resolution. Additionally, public opinion changes over time. Methods for enhancing social dialogue consist mainly of increasing the exchange of information between the two parties, through regular meetings for instance and through social bodies such as economic and social boards (like in France) or pay-body reviews (in the United Kingdom).

In many OECD member countries, tripartite and bipartite institutions help reach an agreement between the government and unions. Bipartite social dialogue covers all exchange of information, consultation, and negotiation between employers and employees without direct government intervention. Tripartite social dialogue opens the discussion to delegates from the government or the ministry of Finance or even to other actors such as consumers' associations for instance. France provides various examples of such tripartite institutions that operate regularly, such as the Economic, Social and Environmental Council, the Employment Advisory Council, the National Commission on Collective Bargaining, and the National Council on Employment, Vocational Training and Orientation. Israel lacks similar institution to prevent disputes or build a path for resolution. Economic and social councils or labour advisory council could be examples of external institutions that may help social dialogue in Israel.

In Israel, Labour Courts, since their creation in 1969, are a partner in social dialogue. Hence, labour courts have become the place where not only legal disputes are solved but also where social agreements between parties are constructed, under the supervision (and often also pressure) of the court.

The Israeli Labour Court System is composed of five Regional Labour Courts, and a higher instance that also serves as an appeals court, the National Labour Court. Regional Labour courts have, in equal numbers, members from labour and from management, sitting with professional judges. In Israel, the right to strike is not covered by the Basic Laws or other statutes but derives from the constitutional freedom of association. However, it is still considered by the courts as having constitutional status, and as a result, the labour courts' reluctance to limit it creates significant difficulty for employers seeking an injunction against a strike. Many public employers feel that the labour courts do not give adequate treatment to collective disputes, especially with regard to requests for injunctions against industrial actions. The Supreme Court is seldom willing to interfere and change the rulings of the National Labour Court (in any case its scope of interference is limited in general, according to previous rulings).

It could be argued that the importance of the judiciary is a symptom of a collapse of norms and trust. In countries where labour relations are based on trust, parties can discuss and negotiate to reach consensus early, strikes are the last resort, and the few strikes that do happen are short and quickly lead to negotiation and agreement – or, in worst-case scenarios, to third-party arbitration. In Israel, this process is lacking and needs to be rebuilt. Assessing the quality of labour relations is challenging, yet it is a key component of a sound collective bargaining system. Effective mediation and arbitration procedures can play an important role in managing conflicts, helping to find an agreement within the framework of collective bargaining and strengthening the public management system.

The labour court is not the optimal solution for sound labour relations. Effective institutions for solving labour disputes would prevent conflicts from taking place, reduce long-lasting strikes, and likely be less costly. Since the institutions for dispute resolution and prevention are lacking, labour courts step in to supervise and manage labour disputes that reach the courts. The courts have the authority and legitimacy that seem to be lacking elsewhere. Labour courts in effect play the role of mediation because no other institution seems to be able to fulfil that essential role.

In Israel, the means to achieve resolution of strikes seem to be common knowledge for all parties (pressure on government to eventually accede to union demands), and therefore one could expect an earlier resolution of the conflict that would avoid bearing this useless cost of strikes and courts. However, since strikes are perceived as the only way to express a demand, the strength of a strike becomes the mean to signal the importance of the social pressure, hence arbitrate between demands. This process is clearly inefficient and an alternative way to initiate social dialogue and reach consensus would improve both public expenses, trust in government and quality of public service delivery.

A fair process of collective bargaining and a sound social dialogue are the best prevention of conflict. Ex ante mechanisms to improve social dialogue are more efficient than ex post conflict resolution mechanisms. Olson's (1988) seminal work on strikes in the public sector showed that strikes are more likely to occur in states without a bargaining law, or without a binding arbitration procedure. However, alternative dispute resolution often requires time; hence, there is a need to elaborate a proper dispute resolution mechanism. Mediation consists of choosing an independent authority that brings the parties to react on an agreement but it lacks the power of implementation and in case of a difficult conflict, it serves only in delaying the dispute resolution. Arbitration entails a third party who examines the dispute or bargaining process, provides data and recommendation and exerts political pressure to negotiate. In this case, again arbitration cannot compel the parties to accept the dispute resolution. Arbitration may also encourage the parties to take extreme positions instead of going toward the middle since the third party will probably propose a middle position. A way to resolve those difficulties is a type of dispute resolution called "final offer arbitration" in which both parties submit a proposal to arbitration and the third party must select one of the two proposals. This encourages the parties to propose a reasonable outcome and converge towards the middle (Carrell and Bales, 2012).

Having a common understanding across social partners is important for building trust and easing the cost of negotiations. Data gathering and joint research between the government, social partners and third parties such as independent research bodies help to build common values, common analysis, and trust. It can be costly to design a reform, by testing new approaches, experimenting with new combinations, and gathering data to do so, however, this initial cost is necessary to increase the level of trust and decrease the cost of negotiations. (see Box 3.6 for a UK example).

In conclusion, the legal and institutional framework for settling negotiations and preventing disputes should be reviewed and reformed. There is no significant alternative labour dispute settlement mechanism that could work without the pressure or a strike or the threat of labour court decisions. All parties willing to renew labour relations in Israel could take part in planning and advancing legislation concerning dispute resolution. Employers and Employees' rights in labour disputes could also be institutionalised.

Transparency and data gathering, joint research between government, unions and third parties can be a starting point to find a common solution and make agreements more sustainable.

Box 3.6. UK: Pay Reviews and Data gathering

In the UK, eight different Pay Reviews Bodies make recommendations on salary adjustments for 2.5 million workers (accounting for about 45% of public sector staff). Each body collects evidence from the employer and trade unions and presents a recommendation to the government concerning pay reforms. The recommendations are not binding, it is up to the Government to decide how to use the information they are presented with. Despite this, an independent and public review helps to ensure that pay reforms are justified and can inform public opinion. In the UK pay reviews help various actors to agree on the description of reality and consequently on solutions to address shortcoming of the pay system. In the UK, pay review bodies have replaced collective bargaining for employees working as school teachers, health workers, armed forces, and prison guards.

Conclusion: Restoring collaborative social dialogue

There seems to be a consensus that the current public sector labour relations arrangements in Israel are not optimal. This, in turn, limits opportunities to design and implement win-win reforms that provide employees with fair pay and employment contracts in return for greater flexibility for the employer (as argued in chapter 2).

The introduction of new technology, in particular, can be an opportunity to renegotiate labour relations and implement win-win reforms. Emerging technologies are an opportunity to rethink labour relations in Israel. Though technologies induce changes in the working conditions and can be considered as a breach of contract by unions, they can be an opportunity to propose a trade-off between payments, training or working hours and technological upgrading. The OECD (OECD, 2019[12]) has highlighted the threats of technological changes but also the opportunities to make labour relations more inclusive, transform the way unions communicate with their members and collaborate to design an inclusive path for growth.

However, in Israel, there is a high level of distrust among social partners in the public sector, and trust is key in successful reforms. The solution is not to abolish unions but to engage them as collaborative social partners in the design of reforms, rather than as opponents to change. Many recent reforms of the public sector failed because of the lack of social dialogue and the ability to build buy-in among employees for the reform's objectives. Building the framework of cooperation and effective social dialogue is crucial to implementing modernisation reforms. Building a capable and professional public service requires the active involvement and engagement of public employees, and hence, sound and stable social dialogue mechanisms.

The morale of public employees and hence their motivation depend on the trust they have in the central government. Reforms could lead either to increasing social conflicts, which seem to be the case in Israel, and which was the case in the USA (in 2011 in Wisconsin and Ohio) or to renewing social dialogue, which has been the case in many European countries including France, Sweden and the Netherlands. Therefore, restoring trust depends on restoring social dialogue.

This is particularly important given the changes introduced in response to the spread of the Covid-19 pandemic – namely the introduction and take up of digital services, and the widespread implementation of remote working. Initially, these changes were designed to protect public sector workers and ensure continuity of service. While the tools provided to CEOs and executives were time-bound, over the longer-term there may be opportunities to embed beneficial elements of this flexibility across the public sector.

For example, during the pandemic, members of the public were encouraged to access public services online rather than in person. This helped limit the spread of the virus, but also presents new opportunities to rethink public service delivery after the crisis. For public sector workers, increased digitalisation has also been a driver of more flexible working patterns, such as remote working. Other elements of flexibility include greater mobility across the public sector, directing resources to where they are most needed. This will require revision of job descriptions and pay structures (as discussed in the previous chapter). Adjustment of working hours and location is another dimension of flexibility that will also require adaptation of performance management frameworks.

These are important steps which stand to increase the effectiveness of public service delivery in routine and crisis situations. Constructive engagement with unions must be a key part of embedding these kinds of positive changes sustainably. Transparency and trust are crucial for an efficient and inclusive government. Building this will require laws, institutions and good will to build sound labour relations. However, changing a social and institutional equilibrium can be very tricky and costly. It is the government's prerogative to initiate a conference to negotiate on labour relations in good faith, with transparency and inclusion: who negotiates, on what, and when. All parties are needed to construct this level of trust and transparency on the outcome. To do so, the government should act to change the rules and institutions that structure social dialog in Israel, and consider the following recommendations.

OECD Recommendations to Improve Israel's Public Sector Bargaining System:

In order to improve Israel's public sector bargaining system and ensure it supports a public service which is forward-looking, flexible and fulfilling to a diverse range of public servants, the Israel government could aim to:

1. **Create institutions for alternative dispute resolution.** The recourse to strike action and number of working days lost indicates a system that does not work for most stakeholders. Developing viable alternatives to strike action is necessary to ensure that strikes are used appropriately – as a tool of last resort. These could include labour relations commissions, or independent arbitration and mediation committees. Broadening the range of tools social partners can use to achieve their aims can help mitigate the need to resort to strike action and thus reduce economic and social disruption.

2. **Protect essential services.** Most OECD countries designate some public services as 'essential' in order to reduce the exposure of citizens to work stoppages. Sometimes the designations can also refer to specific hierarchical levels of the civil service, e.g. top managers. If agreements cannot be reached between employers and unions, alternative dispute resolution mechanisms such as binding arbitration could be explored for essential workers and services. Israel should develop this approach through broad engagement with labour and political leaders, and public debate.

3. **Create affordability constraints.** This would help create a framework of "what's on the table" to improve the bargaining process and safeguard the democratic right of elected governments to allocate public spending based on their political priorities. This could be reinforced through greater separation of the negotiating functions from the budgeting function in the Ministry of Finance while the policy of the budget is discussed and agreed upon within the Ministry of Finance. Israel could also find ways to systematically consider macroeconomic and fiscal indicators, and using these to inform bargaining processes for framework agreements at national level.

4. **Consider options to bring in more employer perspectives to the negotiations:** Collective bargaining should be seen a strategic tool that can be used to improve working conditions in exchange for management reforms to improve e.g. flexibility and/or technological modernisation. This suggests the need to extend the perspective beyond wages, and include line managers and the office/ministry in charge as key partners in the collective bargaining process.

5. **Limit the timing and use of labour disputes:** Israel should consider reviewing and specifying the acceptable conditions for unions to open a dispute during the lifetime of an active agreement. It is important to have a tool to signal disputes and give time for resolution through negotiation and information-exchange. Israel could use or adapt the legal framework to set more specific rules, and an expiry date on notifications of intent to strike. Policies should be reviewed periodically to ensure they are used for the purpose intended.

6. **Unions and public sector management should meet more frequently outside the context of a specific crisis or dispute.** Sharing information, establishing priorities and communicating regularly could help reduce the sense of paralysis and 'winner takes all' mentality that appear to characterise much of labour negotiations in Israel.

7. **The Ministry of Finance should review the scope of topics that are negotiated by Union representatives.** Over time, there appears to have been a blurring of the line between the public sector's duty to consult unions and its obligation to negotiate with unions on certain issues. Unions now have a say on everyday working matters that in many other OECD countries would fall within the remit of managers to resolve. The government of Israel may wish to revise the scope of the concept of "working conditions", find ways to encourage constructive union participation in management reforms and build mutual trust.

8. **Separate line managers from being represented by the same unions as their employees.** When managers are covered by the same collective agreements, they have conflicting interests when negotiating with employees. Israel should set a clear limit to the hierarchical levels that are included in union agreements. Some OECD countries have separate unions to represent the interests of senior-level public servants. Where managers are empowered to manage staff performance, work conditions and engagement, this separation helps ensure objectivity when they make decisions relating to aspects such as pay and workplace relations.

References

Bordogna and Pedersini (2013), *OECD Employment Outlook 2019: The Future of Work*, OECD Publishing, Paris, https://dx.doi.org/10.1787/9ee00155-en. [11]

Cohen, Y. et al. (2007), "The State of Organized Labor in Israel", *Journal of Labour Research*, Vol. 28/2, pp. 255-273, http://dx.doi.org/10.1007/BF03380045. [1]

OECD (2019), *Negotiating Our Way Up: Collective Bargaining in a Changing World of Work*, OECD Publishing, Paris, https://dx.doi.org/10.1787/1fd2da34-en. [10]

OECD (2019), *Negotiating Our Way Up: Collective Bargaining in a Changing World of Work*, OECD Publishing, Paris, https://dx.doi.org/10.1787/1fd2da34-en. [3]

OECD (2019), *Negotiating Our Way Up: Collective Bargaining in a Changing World of Work*, OECD Publishing, Paris, https://dx.doi.org/10.1787/1fd2da34-en. [4]

OECD (2019), *Negotiating Our Way Up: Collective Bargaining in a Changing World of Work*, OECD Publishing, Paris, https://dx.doi.org/10.1787/1fd2da34-en. [5]

OECD (2019), *Negotiating Our Way Up: Collective Bargaining in a Changing World of Work*, OECD Publishing, Paris, https://dx.doi.org/10.1787/1fd2da34-en. [6]

OECD (2019), *Negotiating Our Way Up: Collective Bargaining in a Changing World of Work*, OECD Publishing, Paris, https://dx.doi.org/10.1787/1fd2da34-en. [7]

OECD (2019), *Negotiating Our Way Up: Collective Bargaining in a Changing World of Work*, OECD Publishing, Paris, https://dx.doi.org/10.1787/1fd2da34-en. [8]

OECD (2019), *Negotiating Our Way Up: Collective Bargaining in a Changing World of Work*, OECD Publishing, Paris, https://dx.doi.org/10.1787/1fd2da34-en. [9]

OECD (2019), *OECD Employment Outlook 2019: The Future of Work*, OECD Publishing, Paris, https://dx.doi.org/10.1787/9ee00155-en. [12]

OECD (2018), *Good Jobs for All in a Changing World of Work: The OECD Jobs Strategy*, OECD Publishing, Paris, https://dx.doi.org/10.1787/9789264308817-en. [2]